SHE HE ME

Dayne Bachmann (signature)

DAYNE BACHMANN, LCSW

ISBN: 978-1-64184-730-8 (Paperback)
ISBN: 978-1-64184-731-5 (Ebook)

DEDICATION

First and foremost, this book is dedicated to my spouse for helping to make my hopes and dreams a reality. Thank you for always believing in me. I love you!

This book is also dedicated to my clients past and present. Thank you for putting your trust in me and sharing your stories with me. It has been an honor watching each one of you blossom into your true selves.

ACKNOWLEDGEMENTS

Thank you to the medical practitioners and staff who were instrumental and supported me through all the phases of my journey in becoming my true authentic self.

First, Katherine Tierney, APRN, for your guidance, support and kindness. Thank you, also, for all that you do for our LGBTQ+ community.

Thank you to Dr. Reilly and staff. You were integral to some of the most important aspects of my transition. It is not only for your medical expertise that I am grateful, but also for the acceptance, understanding and care you all extended to me physically, mentally and emotionally while I was in your office. Thank you from the heart.

A debt of gratitude goes to the Short Term Surgery nurses at Griffin Hospital and the nurses and doctors in the operating room. I never once felt I was being judged, and I was treated with the respect everyone deserves. The care I received as a transgender man was nothing short of exceptional.

Thank you, also, to the members of my creative team: Tanya Detrik for being my *"write"*-hand person and Tracy Lutters for your website and cover design expertise and getting me through the associated technical challenges.

Finally, to my beta readers for taking the time out of your busy lives to read and thoughtfully comment on my manuscript.

FOREWORD

I never tire of hearing the stories of real people going through real change. Being your authentic self might be the toughest and most rewarding thing you can do in our culture. There are so many expectations, both internal and external, of how we should be and how we should act. When it comes to gender, there is a prescription for being male or female, and that prescription is handed to you at birth with a lifetime of refills. As a specialist in transgender hormone therapy, I have seen how hundreds of people in my community have navigated those expectations, created space for their authenticity and became themselves when faced with many hurdles. I hit the jackpot in rewarding experiences: I get to hear stories like Dayne's every day.

In these pages, Dayne gives us the gift of vulnerable storytelling of a common experience. He has faced serious trauma and also unexpected grace on his path to being himself, and we are lucky to get to share in that story. There is so much to be learned. Transgender voices are exceedingly important in understanding the transgender experience, and, in this book, we get to hear Dayne both as a transgender person and as a therapist supporting trans patients. It's not always easy to be on your own journey and advocate for your community at the same time, but somehow Dayne has managed both simultaneously. Reading his stories of growing up have only deepened my awe for his ability to not only confidently be himself, but also be an advocate and support system for other transgender people.

Changing, adapting and being true to ourselves is a lifelong journey. Dayne gives us all a deeply personal look inside his experience and transition, and I hope it will leave you as inspired as it did me.

Kathryn S. Tierney, MSN, APRN, FNP-BC, FAANP
Medical Director, Middlesex Health Center for
Gender Medicine and Wellness

INTRODUCTION

I used to have breasts that didn't belong to me. They didn't fit or feel natural. Coming to terms with my body, my feelings about it, my beliefs about myself, the reactions of others and ultimately my resolution to become who I was meant to be—who I am today—has taken the majority of 50 years.

Nearly half of those years involved suffering until I finally discovered that I was not alone in my struggle. The emotional pain and disconnection I had with my body and my identity had a name, a label in the transgender world: dysphoria. According to the American Psychiatric Association, gender dysphoria refers to "psychological distress that results from an incongruence between one's sex assigned at birth and one's gender identity."

My dysphoria, the anxiety, confusion and depression it caused me and all the research, therapy, treatments and surgeries it took to become authentically me, a transgender male, as well as the education to become a therapist who works with gender questioning and transitioning people, has brought my life full circle.

Today, I am happily married to a partner who loves and understands me, having stood by me through my transition. I have a personal passion for my life's work as a therapist who enriches his life by helping other gender-questioning people find theirs.

The prefix "trans" means "across from." In reference to being transgender, it means someone who identifies "across from" their assigned sex from birth. This was true for me, and, ironically, as a therapist, I now sit "across from" others whose paths to authenticity I hope to make smoother than my own.

We are at a time in our culture's history at which definitions and differences matter much more than our sameness. I hope, in some way, sharing my story will help to close that gap.

CONTENTS

THE EARLY YEARS

From a very young age, I knew that something about me, within me, part of me, just didn't feel right, the way I wanted it to, the way I sensed other people naturally seem to feel. I was always uneasy, unsure of what caused me to feel so different, disconnected. As hard as I tried to make sense of it, the pieces of my internal jigsaw puzzle didn't fit the picture on the box.

Looking back, I realize I remember little of my childhood, though recollections come to me in flashes—those moments and events that are vivid. I think that it's because they are of the times the important people in my life pounded me with the messages that something was wrong with me. In different, often trauma-inducing, ways my family and others constantly called attention to it. Their reactions to me made me the outsider. My mere existence irritated them. I angered them. I didn't know why, and it seemed to me they didn't either. I knew I was different. Sometimes, my family's reactions were severe. Often, there was physical assault, always emotional torture—ridicule, beatings even to the extreme of being threatened with a gun to my head… literally.

My parents brought their baby girl home from the hospital with all the related expectations *of* her and *for* her. Who knew?

Until I stopped letting her, my mother chose my outfits, as mothers do. Of course, she most often chose dresses, frilly clothes and all the ribbons and bows to go with them. As I grew old enough to argue, my arguments with my mother revolved around my choices of clothing. She was always cuttingly critical of me for the way I dressed, saying, "Dawn, go change your clothes. They are awful! Why do you always have to look like a slob?"

Regardless of what I was wearing, she criticized me for my unladylike behavior and masculine demeanor. I was endlessly being reminded how I, as a girl, should behave. She relentlessly reprimanded me for anything I did or said that didn't fit the role society attributes to girls—sit like a girl, be sweet like a girl, girls don't get dirty, girls like dolls and tea parties, not trucks and baseball, and on and on.

What I had to face each day could not have gotten worse than being raised as a Catholic. I always felt guilty, even though I didn't know why. I was always waiting to be accused of some wrongdoing, even though I hadn't done anything wrong. I feared that, in the eyes of my parents and God, there was something really wrong with me, and, whatever it was, it wasn't okay to be me. Those beliefs rooted themselves in me as tormentors of my deepest fears. I was a sinner, condemned in the eyes of the church, devoid of God's grace. I felt so much shame and guilt for something I could not explain.

I was angry, too, when I discovered girls couldn't be altar boys. What?! Only boys were allowed to serve at the altar in the Catholic Church, but not me? *What do you mean! That is just not fair!* Like so many other girls, most of whom never recognized the injustice or cared about the inherent double standard, I had to sit in church on Sundays and watch boys honor the Lord when I couldn't, simply because of my gender. It was one more reason I felt disconnected from my faith. I ended up hating religion and church.

My social awareness of my differences started for me in kindergarten. Simply having to form two lines according to gender confused me and added to my feeling I was separate. I was emotionally out of line, regardless of which one it was. I think that's when I stepped onto the island that became my lonely and uncomfortable home for so many years.

I attended Catholic school from first through eighth grade. That's when I really felt the confusion of "God is a loving god, and God is a punishing god." Nuns, teachers and my parents repeated those messages. What my guilt did was make this a hell on earth because I was always hearing, "God is going to punish you for that," when I screwed up, and "See? God punished you!" when adults wanted me to suffer the consequences of my actions.

I could not escape the fear of discovery (of exactly what, I was not yet sure). The school uniforms were also my tormenters. The very definition of the word "uniform" means, "the same," and I was not. I wore the prescribed uniform, a girl's jumper, but I envied the boys in their shirts and ties. Public school would have been kinder, maybe.

I never got good grades in school. I scraped by in all of my subjects, because I just couldn't focus on anything for very long, even if I loved the subject. The subjects I hated were even more elusive. Frankly, in retrospect, I don't know how I got through at all. It didn't help to be constantly told by my mom and teachers that my grades were suffering because I was just lazy. "You just don't apply yourself," they chided me.

I realize, now, that under my emotional circumstances, I was actually doing the best I could, but, of course, no one understood that, not even me.

When not at school, I played with the neighborhood boys. I felt like one of them, and I was just as tough as they were. I was most comfortable in jeans, tee-shirts and baseball hats, which my mother hated. I loved getting dirty and playing football and Whiffle ball. The boys accepted me. On the outside, I was a tomboy, a label that rough and tumble little girls can often get away with during their pre-teen years. Just a stage, most would say, but mine was not just a stage. Or perhaps it was a stage in my young life in which others could accept me, if I couldn't wholly accept myself.

Birthday parties at that age were mostly for other girls. I always had to make the choice to pretend to fit in. To me, it felt more like Halloween, with the need to wear a mask that didn't give away who I really was.

I wanted to play in team sports, like Little League. Back then, that wasn't allowed, and my family was happy to remind me it was for boys only. I knew I was born to be physically adventurous, daring and different from what they expected of a girl. I didn't feel like a girl, even though I didn't really know what that feeling was. Without being able to communicate it, I knew somehow it wasn't me. I continually questioned whether I was born into the right body. My brother had a penis. That gave him the ability to stand up while peeing. I was jealous. It confused me. Why couldn't I?

So often, I would go to sleep at night praying to wake up the next day as a boy.

* * *

At some point in early middle school days, most young girls have crushes on boys. I did, or so I thought. There was something magnetic about boys. I fixated on them. I was fascinated, attracted to their behavior. I wanted to be around them. It felt natural to me. I understood how they behaved, what they did and what they liked. I am sure that others who observed me thought my pre-teen attraction to boys was just typical for a girl. Even this typically female behavior felt strange to me.

Those feelings soon led me to question myself and my underlying intentions. What I finally realized was my feelings about boys weren't about the attraction to the opposite sex. I did not have what would normally be a crush, but actually it was a deep longing to be like them. I think I confused the attraction with affinity.

Whatever it was, I was miserable mostly all the time. Uncomfortable in my own skin. I stuffed my anger in silence. I thought I was just an angry person; anger was who I was. I had nothing to compare it to, no way to differentiate it, no way to explain. I didn't know there were words for what I was feeling. It was just me, and I couldn't escape me.

I struggled in isolation. I always felt disconnected from family, friends and the world. I saw or knew no one—no boys, men, girls or women in the world—who were like me. I had no role model for the person trapped inside me. I didn't know that anyone else like me even existed. I lived in quiet desperation. I didn't even know what I'd say if I had someone to listen. Again, it felt like I was on my own island, and there was no bridge that connected me to the rest of the world. I was stuck in nowhere land without even so much as a compass. Frustration and despair ruled my life. I often just escaped reality by watching television. It helped me shut down my thoughts, feelings and emotions.

One temporary escape and bittersweet memory was watching The Brady Bunch. I loved it so much because I got to see what a real family could be. With that, I wished and prayed for a family like that, and constantly wondered and dreamed of what it would be like to have a loving, accepting family. Now, I often wonder how different my life would have been, how different I might have been, if I had received the love, encouragement and support I craved. All I wanted was to be accepted. I longed to belong and be valued by my family and others.

Like many pre-teens, I spent a lot of my time in my room, listening to music to escape from reality and my family. It was 1983, and singer Rick Springfield was on the charts. I especially loved his song, "Human Touch." It was a song on the track of his "Living in Oz" album. Funny, I guess I was living in my version of Oz, dumped in a strange land, struggling to find my way home, without the cohorts and support that Dorothy found there. Though they weren't my style, I might have actually worn and cherished those girly ruby slippers if I thought they could take me home to me.

The lyrics of Springfield's song tell how, in the world's craziness, we all need the human touch. That song sang my heart. The lyrics and pounding beat deeply resonated with my intense longing for something I could only imagine—myself. What would it be like to feel love and affection from a parent? A hug? A pat on the back? Reassurance they cared about me or my feelings? That somehow they were proud of me for something, or anything? Some simple encouragement? Acceptance, at the very least.

I was a pressure cooker of anger and anxiety, except in odd moments when I couldn't contain it. When I did erupt, it wasn't anything serious that provoked it. My inappropriate overreaction made me more misunderstood, both to myself and anyone else in proximity. I once punched a friend in the face because she said something I didn't like. I can't remember what she said, but I even surprised myself with my reaction. That episode got me suspended from school. My mother was not happy. And, at that time, I imagined God wasn't pleased either, which made it all the worse.

Actually, my mother was angry because she didn't want me home all day. In her opinion, she saw suspension as the school rewarding me for bad behavior. She felt my behavior at school was the school's responsibility. *They* should have to deal with the punishment for me, not *her*. In her eyes, a few days at home was not the answer. So, she called the school to tell them they'd better expect me the next day. She said she didn't care if they made me clean toilets or church pews, but I could not sit home and enjoy a few days of "vacation." I went to school the next day.

* * *

Puberty raises hell for most adolescents. The hormones, body changes, social scrutiny, feelings and changes in relationships are difficult, distressing or, at the very least, unsettling. For me, being unable to find words for what I was feeling was frustrating. I knew I was different, and I hated it. In the absence of any feeling of belonging, the disconnection isolated me, and longing and deep sadness became my emotional prison.

Being a girl, I knew bodily changes were coming. I just tried to ignore them. I didn't want to become more female than I already was. So, when I reached puberty, I was horrified. Growing breasts and having my period were devastating, and that fueled even more anger that landed me in deep despair. The entire menstruation process and what it meant was like an invasion of my body. I didn't want to be a female; I certainly didn't want all that went with it.

To make things horribly and embarrassingly worse, my mother found it necessary to tell my father that his daughter had officially entered womanhood. That would be awful enough for any young woman. For me, it was a betrayal not only of my privacy but my entire being. The mere term "womanhood" made me feel like dying. I ached for a male body.

I could no longer ignore what was happening, and the discomfort within me and the betrayal that was my body grew even stronger, making me even more uncomfortable than ever to be trapped in a body that didn't belong to me. I hated my breasts. They were always in the way. I didn't want to wear a bra or even show that I had breasts. I wore loose clothing as my disguise. As my breasts grew, so did my tools of disguise.

As a young teen, I would go swimming at the YMCA with a friend. She often protested when I went into a bathroom stall to change clothes instead of staying in the locker room with the other females. I remember feeling so uncomfortable undressing. I just didn't belong there. My friend would question my need for privacy, commenting that we all had the same "equipment." For me, it was a different type of embarrassment than other young girls might experience. Mine was extreme self-consciousness in having body parts that weren't really in tune with who I really was. It was the same in gym class. I ended up not going at all.

Despite my wishes, I had inherited the dark hair gene of my Italian lineage, which, in my puberty, became the undeniable body hair that went with it. It didn't take long for the other kids to notice. They openly ridiculed me for having facial hair and hairy arms and legs. With that, one thought continuously plagued me: *How am I supposed to play the role of a girl if I have all this body hair?* I wished it would just go away, and I prayed I would wake up and it would be gone.

FAMILY

It was my family who bullied me, not my peers.
My father was an abusive person. He was not at
home very often during my childhood. When he
wasn't working, it was common knowledge that, more
often than not, he was out cheating on my mom. When
he was at home, I learned very early in life to tread
lightly around the landmines of his anger to hedge off
his subsequent abuse. The uncertainty of his volatility
lacked any discernible logic. Anything and even nothing—just seeing me could set him off. Waiting to see
how his anger would burst was frightening. Objects and
obscenities would fly at me. Verbal abuse was a kindness.

The rooms in our house were laid out in a circle
that formed the perfect chase-track, him in pursuit
of me. I vividly remember one of the many times he
caught me. I can't remember what provoked him, but
he came after me, yelling, "What the hell is wrong
with you?" I outran him until he cornered me in my
bedroom. Catching me from behind, his hand met my
back. The force of the assault sent me sprawling on to
the bed. I was grateful it was there to cushion my fall.
The stinging red outline of his hand was imprinted on
my back for a week. It was so painful, the pressure of

my shirt against my back, that it kept me from being able to lean back on my chair at school. The handprint healed; the memory is still a wound.

More painful than even his abuse of me was that my mother would not defend or protect me. Instead, she made me apologize to him for making him angry, as if his abuse of me was my fault. In fact, shortly after the handprint episode, my parents told me I was a delinquent, and they were planning to put me in a juvenile residential program in a nearby town. I wondered how they could even think of sending me away to such a horrible place. Had they been planning this? For how long? What was wrong with me? What made them think of me this way? They did not send me, but the threat hung over me for a long time afterwards.

Other relatives bullied me, too. My family made a practice of bullying anyone who was different. My maternal uncle Frank was the worst offender. He continually harassed my cousin, who was overweight, had excessive facial hair, was shy and intellectually challenged. She was petrified for a good cause. She would cower at the sight of him, attempting to be invisible.

While my cousin endured Frank's insults, I was his favorite target. Frank was like a pit bull. If he grabbed onto you, he just wouldn't let go. He would call me names and ridicule me and my appearance, declaring that I was fat; I needed a tentmaker to make my clothes; I was so big I should have "Wide Load" printed on my backside.

The only thing anyone would say to him was, "Oh, Frank, knock it off." No one would come to my defense or do anything to protect me.

When I look back at pictures of myself from that time in my life, I see I was not overweight. I didn't deserve it. Still, the scars of his bullying live on in me, and to this day I am ever conscious and sensitive about my weight.

This is the same uncle who pointed a gun at me twice. The first time I was a kid. It was a Sunday morning. My mother, grandmother, brother and I were in the car about to pull out of the garage on our way to church. Besides the overhead garage door, there was a regular door on the side of the garage that led out to the sidewalk. It was open, and through it I could see my uncle Frank standing on the sidewalk holding his gun, which was pointed at us in the car. Fish in a barrel we were. *Oh My God!* I flung myself down, diving onto the car floor. *We gotta get outta here.* Above the sound of blood rushing in my ears, I heard my grandmother's whimper and my mother choking back a squeal of fear as she drove out of the garage and away as quickly as possible.

Not a word was said about the incident on the way to church or after. When we got to church, I sat there thinking, *I guess we're not supposed to talk about this stuff.* The only comfort was the candy I could always count on from my grandmother to get me through church.

The second time Frank threatened my life with a gun was when I was an adult in my 30s. I was visiting him and my aunt one summer day. It was hot, and they had an inground pool. It was clear from his behavior that Frank was in a disturbingly foul mood. He was pacing in and out of the house. He kept it up for a time, maybe 30 minutes. Then he appeared with a gun in his hand. He walked directly toward the pool, his gaze fixed on me. He was only six feet from me when I ducked underwater, like that would save me. When I came up for air, he was still there. I went under again. Each time I rose to the top for air, I heard him laughing at me, amused by this sick and dangerous game. His wife began shrieking, "Knock it off Frank! Knock it off!" He didn't move. What could I do? I was helpless, and no one came to my rescue. Eventually, he relaxed his aim, turned and disappeared into the house.

Frank passed away several years ago. He'd had several terrible marriages, and his three children disowned him when they were old enough to make that choice. What gnaws at my core is questioning what caused him to be like that and, specifically, so openly hateful toward me more than anyone else in the family. Did my gender confusion somehow impact him? I don't know and never will.

Over the years, I realized these bullies were the outspoken members of my family, so no one challenged them. I was outspoken in my own way, which may have gotten me more negative attention. I voiced my opinions because I figured I had nothing to lose. If I was going to have a gun to my head anyway, I might as well speak up. I felt if I stayed quiet, it meant I accepted their opinions and behavior, which made me just like them. I didn't want to be like them, a person who judged others. I knew too well what that felt like. I didn't want to attack others for what they looked like, who they were with or the color of their skin. I refused to keep my opinions to myself. I think I learned some of that from my grandmother, Frank's mother. She knew when to challenge him and when to back off. In talking back (when there wasn't a gun present), I was trying to stand up for myself, because I saw the alternative as a horrific dead end, anyway.

HIGH SCHOOL

It came time to decide which high school curriculum to choose—college courses or business courses. I knew many families who encouraged their daughter's confidence in the process of their career choice and, if appropriate, their choice of school. They wanted them to be happy and successful. Not my parents. I said that I thought I'd like to be a mechanic when I graduated. I was told, "That is a man's job! Your hands will always be filthy! Girls do not want hands that are ugly and filthy!"

My other thought was to enlist in the military. Then I heard, "You're crazy. Women don't go into the service! You could never make it through boot camp. You will get married. Your husband will support you, and you will have kids and take care of your family! You need to take business classes, because you are not going to college." Though, to my surprise, I discovered later that my parents had put money away for my college education.

Even as I was growing up, two of my aunts would ask about my plans, suggesting a career as a flight attendant or nurse. One of them was actually the school nurse at my high school.

I chose the business route, and I took a nurse's aide class taught by my aunt. After taking the class, she encouraged me to continue a nursing education. I may have liked the idea, but I rebelled without giving it a thought. Besides, my grades weren't up to the task.

I hated high school. I went there to see my friends. I walked to school, and I began each day by filling my thermos, not with coffee, but with vodka and orange juice. Before school, I would meet up with friends in the woods just on the perimeter of the school grounds, where we would smoke pot. These friends were the people I felt most comfortable with. I did not judge them or feel judged by them. We were all black sheep in our own ways. That was some comfort. I escaped the reality of school with alcohol, marijuana and unfulfilling relationships. I graduated, just barely.

Because of all the pressure to accept a traditional female role, I tried to live it. It might have made me a bit more acceptable from the outside, but on the inside I knew it was a lie. Once again, I thought if I was only relegated to my family's choices for me, I would be better off dead. Their opinions imprisoned me. I was so hopelessly desperate I thought about suicide.

These thoughts actually started when I was 14 years old with the desire to escape my female body, and how good it would be not to wake up in the morning. By the time I graduated from high school, I had a plan. When I was told that my goal in life should be to find a man to take care of me and have children, I believed I was headed for a life of nothing—I would *be* nothing, *have* nothing, *do* nothing and *amount* to nothing if I didn't do what my family told me to do. It was not what I wanted, but I couldn't escape, so what was the point? I would be better off dead.

I thought about suicide. And I planned it.

If you call a suicide hotline, they ask you a series of questions. Your answers are significant indicators of your level of intention. One such question is, "Do you have a plan?" Meaning, have you planned how you will kill yourself? I had a plan. I knew the exact tree I was going to crash my car into. I drove by that tree every day. Every day as I approached it, I wondered, *will this be the day*? Every day, something stopped me. That made me so angry. "I really am such a loser," I thought. "I can't even commit suicide. What is wrong with me?"

Of course, I lived despite my plans.

You have to be desperate to plan your own death. I was really struggling with being female. Yet, I had no idea what to do about it. How do I go on? I didn't hit that tree. Was I a coward or was there something in me that just couldn't give up? I didn't really believe in miracles, but I wanted one. I was fighting me, and, in a strange way, I won the battle, but there was still the war waging inside of me.

It was in high school I first encountered gays. I don't remember when I learned what it meant to be a lesbian or a gay male. I am guessing it might have filtered through my unconscious awareness having overheard comments at home. My entire upbringing was peppered with hearing my parents and extended family use derogatory language when referring to black people, gay people and literally anyone who was some-how different than they were. All of it was always judgmental and cruel.

16

I remember hearing my womanizing father joking with his like-minded friend about the friend's experience in picking up an attractive female hitchhiker. Having gotten her in the car, he proceeded to make a sexual advance toward her only to discover she was actually transgender. The fact that he had fallen for her didn't matter; the joke was always a never-ending cruel slander directed toward her.

My discovery of lesbians and gay males in school led me to the conclusion that I must be lesbian. Choosing to identify as a lesbian was solely because I never had the words to describe how I differed from other women. Being lesbian fit some feelings I had. I embraced the label and cut my hair very short. I started dating girls. They merely considered me a "butch lesbian," which meant there was nothing feminine about me.

I still felt confused, but this new label also gave me relief, freedom and a sense of empowerment. This was a huge step forward in what it felt like to discover the real me. Having found a label for myself and a "tribe" of my own made me happy.

Then came the day I came out to my mother. It was a day filled with thunder, lightning and raging downpours, a foreshadowing of what was to come for me.

"Are you crazy?!" My mother roared through the house as she ripped the clothes from my closet and threw them out the second-floor window onto the sopping wet lawn. "Don't think you are living under my roof! Get out! Find somewhere else to live, because you are not staying here!"

Outside, I attempted to gather up all my dripping belongings from the muddy lawn. How could this be? God, what did I do to deserve this? I stood in the grass wondering how God could punish me just for not being what everyone wanted me to be. How could my mother throw me out with such violence for telling her my truth?

ON MY OWN

I did not hear from my mother for more than a year after that day. My heart could not understand how she could be so ashamed of me, of having a gay child.

I had to figure out life quickly. It was a struggle both financially and emotionally. I moved in with a friend, then another somewhere else. Nothing felt like home.

I was working in a gas station, and I also worked as a Certified Nurse's Aide for several years. When I finally I got my own apartment, there were times I had to rely on food pantries, and I often received shut-off notices from the utility companies.

I fell in and out of relationships, looking to fill the emptiness in me. None of them did. I kept searching, to no avail.

Also, at that time, I was looking for a social outlet. I decided that softball, being part of a team, might be a good place to connect. I joined a local women's softball team. After the games, we always headed to a local bar. By this time, I'd stopped drinking, but I went anyway to socialize. There were a lot of strong and positive women in that group. While I formed some good relationships, and some of them are still friends today, I also realized hanging out with the lesbian crowd didn't fit me either.

I suppose that realization threw me into another form of identity crisis. I was eighteen years old, a rejected child and a gender-confused person trying to become an independent and responsible adult. I was emotionally overloaded and financially under-supported. I think that's what provoked my first panic attack.

I was in the grocery store, just standing in the checkout line. Suddenly, an inexplicable, intense fear overcame me. I didn't know what was happening. I really thought I was going to die. I felt the fear of an imminent danger I couldn't rationalize. My heart raced, and I was sweating and trembling, which quickly became full-body shaking. My throat constricted until I couldn't breathe. I was sweating and having chills at the same time. I was about to lose control so I fled, leaving the cart right where it was. I ran as fast as I could out the door. The air felt good on my flushed face as I raced back to my car. I sat there in my car for what seemed like hours, waiting to regain my composure. Finally, I drove home. After that, anxiety plagued me daily. The mere thought that an attack like that could happen sent me into hiding.

At that time, I was living with Caroline, a sixty-year-old woman I'd met at Alcoholics Anonymous. It turns out I didn't actually have a drinking problem. I was just drinking to numb my feelings. When Caroline discovered I was in need of a place to live, she offered me a room, one of the two she rented to interns of the nearby hospital.

The couch became my best friend—the safe haven it had always been. I knew I didn't want to see or talk to anyone. I just wanted to be alone, to escape the world. The thought of going out terrified me. I was so afraid of another panic attack and what might happen in life outside, I just hid inside.

Staying in didn't stop the anxiety, though. It manifested in physical form from my place on the couch and began to affect my appetite. Very quickly, I was unable to eat. When I tried to force myself to eat something, I literally choked. Another type of panic attack overtook me. I couldn't swallow, not any kind of food at all, not even the things I loved to eat. I would choke and have to spit things out.

I was scared out of my mind. What was happening to me? If you don't eat, you die. I might have thought I wanted that, but this was real. Frightening. I knew I could not go on this way. But I was helpless. Why couldn't I help myself?

I couldn't eat or get off the sofa. I was as phobic about going out as a person who can't stand on a roof or fly in a plane. I couldn't stay shut in forever, but I couldn't bear the thought of taking one step outside of the house. Deep down, I knew I had to.

It was Caroline who kept at me, insisting that I had to eat. I don't know what would have happened otherwise. I probably would have ended up in the psych ward, or at least in the hospital. I feared both.

She would take me to the grocery store to get ice cream and then take me back to her house to sit with me until I ate. I gagged at the thought of food, but Caroline kept at it with me. I finally could tolerate soft, smooth food like ice cream. I started with a small spoonful of what had always been my favorite flavor and made slow progress from there. All the while she sat with me, offering support, keeping me accountable for each difficult swallow.

It took almost six months of nurturing from Caroline to conquer my eating disorder, one spoonful at a time. During this time, I lost a lot of weight. I would have thought that my family might have liked that after how they had ridiculed me for so long about being overweight when I wasn't. It turns out that, after dropping two pant sizes, all my mother could say to me was, "You're too thin!" Yet, she showed no curiosity or concern for why I'd lost so much weight.

I was struggling with panic attacks. The fear of them reoccurring was as scary as the attacks themselves. The anxiety kept me depleted and unable to function. Underneath it all was the struggle with my identity. As it turns out, I kept at it, and I thank Caroline for that. Who knows what would have happened to me otherwise? It took time, but, with her help, I got myself off the sofa, found work and got on with my life.

I continued to live with Caroline for a few more years. She was a very positive, caring person and a major influence in my life. She had what I came to realize was moral character. This was something I had never seen or experienced in my family of origin. As it turns out, I might have stayed at Caroline's home longer were it not for those values of hers! Despite what I was learning from her, I had gotten into a relation-ship with a married woman. The circumstance of my relationship was not acceptable to Caroline's lifestyle. She gave me an ultimatum—end the relationship and stay, or leave. I was young, stupid and stubborn. I left.

For as long as I could remember, I longed for good, loving relationships. I knew they existed, but I had no role model, no example to follow. I am not sure I even knew then what they looked like. Caroline taught me who I had to be to have a good relationship. She was my role model for a caring relationship. I came to realize how she filled the role of surrogate mother for me when I needed to be cared for. I honor her memory with my tattoo of the Alzheimer's ribbon surrounded by forget me not flowers imprinted on my arm.

During that time in my life, none of my employment was leading anywhere except to the next paycheck. I had a variety of jobs, including gas station attendant and nursing assistant in a nursing home. I enjoyed working with the elderly, and helping them made me like myself more. Once again, I considered nursing, but, having goofed off in high school, I didn't have the grades, anyway. My mother knew that and told me if I straightened up I could have the tuition money my parents put away for me. As it turns out, there was none; my father had stolen it for his own use.

Eventually, I got a job as a secretary to a guy whose business was automobile damage appraisals. He would assess the cost to repair cars that had been in accidents. I worked there for three years. He was a great boss who knew how to treat his employees with kindness and respect. He taught me about the business and how to manage employees.

What I learned while working there made me think that maybe becoming an appraiser like he was would be a good fit for me. I thought I had finally found something that might offer me some kind of stable profession. When I brought the idea up to my boss, his response was, "Females have a really tough time in this industry. I think I only know one woman who does this. The men at the body shops give her a really hard time." I don't think he was being cruel; I think he was genuinely concerned for me. Discouraged, I took his word for it and let the idea die.

GRANDPARENTS

In 1994, my maternal grandfather, Frank, died. I was 24 years old, and his death hit me hard. He was the man I looked up to, and his death was my first experience with losing a loved one who was important to me.

My grandparents' house was right next door to ours. It was a safe and sane haven. When things at my house became volatile, there was a retreat for me just next door with my grandparents. What I didn't realize for a long time was that my grandmother was always monitoring what I was doing. I found this out one day when I caught her watching me from her kitchen window. As a kid, I figured she was just spying on me. As an adult, I realized she was actually looking out for me in a way my parents didn't. It finally made sense why everyone seemed to always know what I was up to.

My grandparents' home served as a calm oasis of acceptance and kindness for me. They were loving in the way they treated me. Unlike at my house, they said nothing negative about anyone, including me. If there was something they didn't like, they addressed it directly to your face, instead of talking behind your back. People always knew where they stood with them, including me.

Sometimes as a child, I would sleep over at my grandparents' house. Even though it was just next door, it was a great escape for me. My grandmother and I would watch some of our favorite television shows together. I'd go to bed around 10 p.m., but I would lie awake until after the 11 o'clock news waiting for her to go to bed. I felt safer and slept better just knowing she was across the hall from me.

Growing up, my grandfather was my male role model. Like my grandmother, he loved and nurtured me. And, unlike my father, my grandfather never criticized me. In fact, he was one of my greatest supporters.

He taught me a lot, and I was always attentive, learning all I could from him. I paid attention to how he took care of his home, possessions and my grandmother. From him, I learned how women deserved to be treated, how to replace a leaky faucet, take care of a lawn and countless building and life maintenance lessons. These are things I draw on today. As much as I paid attention to what he did, I also paid attention to *how* he did what he did. He took the time and effort to explain and teach me. In each lesson, be it yard work or fixing things around the house, he taught me how to work smarter, not harder.

I trusted my grandfather, and I knew I could lean on him if I needed to, but I never did.

He was a smoker and eventually developed emphysema. After that, heavy work like mowing the lawn, raking leaves and shoveling snow became too difficult for him. They left these chores for me. He would watch from the kitchen window, never failing to yell out his instructions for how to get the job done right with the least amount of effort.

When it was time for my driving lessons, it was my grandfather who took me out driving. I can still picture him beside me, the gentle gruff of his words, "Check your mirrors," or "Watch out now for that kid up there on the bike."

The year after he died, my parents got divorced. I don't know why it took my mother so long to decide to divorce him. He abused her and all of us, and it was a commonly known fact that he continually ran around with other women. Mom's news came as a surprise to me, simply because she didn't tell me anything until the day it was final. I had no clue she had filed for divorce. I should not have been surprised, because keeping secrets was just a way of life with my family. At least, the arguments and out-and-out fights between my parents were finally over.

* * *

"Your grandmother has lung cancer." My mother delivered the news to me despite my grandmother's plea not to. She knew how upset I would be. It devastated me.

"You must not tell my granddaughter," she told my mother. My mother made me promise not to let my grandmother know I knew, but that kind of secret can't remain hidden for very long. Even though she didn't want me to worry, I couldn't ignore that my "Sunshine" was ill.

It was 2001, and by this time I had had very little contact with my family, except for my relationship with my grandmother. She was always accepting of me, regardless of my life choices.

We had become even closer after my grandfather passed. I checked in on her daily. She was a strong woman, but I think losing my grandfather broke her heart, and seeing her cry broke mine. There was so little I could do to ease her grief. I wanted to be there for her the way she was always there for me.

I called or visited her every day. It helped me as much as it did her. She was sunshine to my soul, and that's when I began to call her "Sunshine," my pet name for her.

From then on, I always greeted her with, "Hello, Sunshine." I visited her as often as possible but, at the very least, wouldn't miss at least calling her every day. Often, she'd answer the phone with feigned annoyance, as if I was bothering her, saying, "What do you want now?!" We'd laugh and exchange details of the day.

My grandmother loved bingo and was an avid player. This was one thing I could do for her. Off we would go on the short drive to our weekly bingo dates at the church hall. All the while, I knew she was powering through the pain she was experiencing. Getting her in and out of the car was the most challenging part of the trip for her physically, knowing that it was equally difficult for me. Finally, one evening, she told me the outings had become too much for her to handle. I remember that night and the look on her face when she told me. Anger at cancer rises in me every time I think of it. I felt so helpless against the disease and the trauma it caused her. All I could do was be with her.

When she could no longer stay in her own home, I put aside the deep hurt and anger of my childhood years, and, for the next few months, I moved back in with my mother in order to help care for my grandmother.

She went into hospice care in May 2001 and passed after only a few days there. It was my second and most devastating loss.

In the days following her death, I was planting flowers in her yard. As I sat in the dirt, a butterfly landed right next to me. It stayed there with me for a long time. I knew it was a sign. It was then I became a believer in signs.

It was only after she passed I learned more about her life. While going through her belongings, I found a Western Union letter, dated November 8, 1944, from The Secretary of War expressing deep regret that my grandfather was missing in action in Italy. My heart sank when I read that. I could only imagine how she must have felt. Then there was a follow-up letter dated a few months later reporting he was safe and in the hospital.

She was the foundation of support to the family through so many of their challenges with illness, financial hardships, alcoholism, divorces, abusive relationships, legal problems and more. I understood for the first time how her experiences were the source of her compassion, when so many other people would have been judgmental.

I was the only grandchild who maintained a relationship with her. I learned a lot from her by how she lived each day, regardless of circumstances. My grandmother gifted me one of the most powerful lessons of my life, to see beyond a person's outward appearance and even inappropriate behavior. She made me aware of how important it is to look beyond the labels others might brand us with. What is inside of us is what is important, even in me. I had to learn from that to be compassionate toward myself. Until I did, her love comforted the tender places in me that others tried to destroy.

It is no surprise that my grandmother's actual name was Grace. I keep her spirit with me in the tattoos on my arms that are symbols of my love for her—the Chinese symbol for grace surrounded by forget me not flowers; a cardinal feather with the words "kindness, live, love, laugh, breathe" inside it; a cross, a few butterflies and the musical notes to the song, "You are my Sunshine."

TERRY

After my grandmother passed, I lost direction in my life or realized I never had one. She acted as true north on the compass of my life, even though I might not have realized it. Without that I wondered, *What should I do now? What can I do? Where do I go from here? How do I get there?*

This quandary led me to take stock of my adult life. It presented a dismal track record. I was still living at my mother's house, and, for my own well-being, I couldn't remain living there. Before moving back to care for my grandmother, I'd had several apartments, though I often just scraped by financially, often relying on food banks for food. In dire times, when I couldn't afford rent, I couch surfed. I had jobs but no career or even any career aspirations. I reviewed the many meaningless relationships I'd had with sadness.

I think my mother recognized my vulnerability and, as such, saw it as an opportunity. Still really unable to accept me as a lesbian, she took advantage of my situation and repeated what I'd always heard in my youth, "You will have nothing and get nowhere in life if you don't get married. You need a man to support you."

Could she be right? Maybe she was. To this point, everything I tried failed to make me happy. I considered the idea. Regardless of how I tried, my life was still a mess. I was tired of it. It was a quintessential example of the adage about insanity—doing the same thing over and over and expecting different results. Maybe it was time for something different. A relationship with a man. Could that be the answer?

The idea of having someone to support me financially was enticing. What a relief it could be. Maybe I could just try dating a man? Just try it, no promises. I wasn't convinced, but, from a place of despair, I considered the idea.

Over time, my mother's nagging wore me down. I moved out of her home and got my own apartment. I literally hung up my baseball hat, shoved my lesbian label back in the closet and went out shopping for more feminine clothes.

Then I joined Match.com.

It didn't take long to connect with Terry, who was in the Army, stationed in Iraq. When I discovered that his stateside home was right in the town next to mine, I thought it might be a cosmic sign that this could be right for me.

In the service, Terry didn't have easy access to a computer, so the relationship continued with writing letters and talking on the phone about once per month. That is how we stayed connected long distance until he came home almost a year later. Of course, my mother was over-the-moon excited, and that kept her off my back.

I finally met Terry in person when he returned to the states from Iraq in the spring of 2004. I felt he had not misrepresented himself. He was authentically the person I had come to know from our correspondence. All in all, I thought that could be enough for me. We married and were miserable, but I felt I had to stay in the marriage for so many reasons. I was stuck in a charade because I believed it was what I was supposed to do—get married and have children.

Shortly after the wedding, Terry got shipped off to Iraq again. He spent the majority of our marriage overseas. That was a huge relief for me. The only time I felt calm was when he was away. Each time he came home, I begged him to re-enlist. I told him if he didn't we were going to get divorced. So, he went over to Iraq again.

I knew I was being selfish, and I felt somewhat guilty, but it was the only way I could deal with the charade of a marriage. I never wanted to be married to a man. When he wasn't around, I could forget him, along with the pressure of trying to be who everyone expected me to be.

When he came home, I felt like a caged animal. My anger was always just below the surface, and any little thing could make it erupt. I actually became abusive. It's not an excuse, but, having grown up as I did, I was exhibiting all the bad behaviors I had learned from my family. I wasn't proud of that. I can't even recall any civil conversations between the two of us. I could see my verbal attacks hurt him to the core, and, in my own experience, I knew that kind of pain would last so much longer than a physical bruise, though I inflicted those as well. One time, a misguided swing of my backpack connected with his head instead of his arm and knocked him out cold. I was terrified I'd killed him. And, still, almost any object within my reach could quickly become a weapon. We were both miserable, and, over time, he became just as abusive toward me.

I was especially angry with my mother for convincing me I was nothing and would be nothing without a husband. I was so frustrated I drank, attempting to gulp some relief. I didn't know what else to do. I couldn't come to terms with what I was feeling, and I couldn't share my feelings.

Though all of this dysfunctional behavior went on for seven years, there were some benefits to being married to Terry. The biggest one was having his financial support.

There was the added pressure on me to look and behave as a wife. Since my teen years, I had longed to have hair removal but could never afford it. Having the benefit of Terry's income, I could finally do it.

Also, I wanted an education that would allow me to work in some true profession. I resented my family's insistence that a girl like me didn't need a college education and how they had disparaged every career path I might have dared to imagine for myself. I hated that I never had the option to go to college, since, thanks to my father, even the "someday if you straighten up" promise of tuition was spent. I decided that being married to Terry was my golden opportunity, and I was going to take it. As his spouse, the Army would pay for me to get a degree. I decided to pursue social work.

In 2006, at 36 years of age, I got my shit together. Despite my having hated high school and being discouraged about my academic abilities, I enrolled in the local community college. I would pursue my calling and maybe have the satisfaction of showing my family how wrong they were about me.

That same year, I transferred to Southern Connecticut State University to pursue a bachelor's degree in social work. My educational goals were the real reason I stayed married to Terry for as long as I did. Embarrassing, but true. Yes, I took advantage of Terry's Army career, and of Terry as well. I am ashamed of that.

While I am grateful to have the education, it turns out that, to this day, some of my choices are still costing me plenty. I took the money from the Army that was meant for my tuition, and I spent it so I didn't have to work while going to school full-time. Had I paid my student loans with it, I would not be paying today on the significant student loan debt I still have.

THERAPY

In 2007, while going to college, I sought therapy. This was a tremendous step for me. I was wary, but I found a therapist. At our first meeting, I asked how long the process was going to take. I was serious, and she knew better than to give me a straight answer. I stayed, figuring I'd finish within a few months.

I went faithfully every week for many months. It was eye opening for me and ultimately life changing. Following her lead, I struggled through processing enough of my childhood trauma to unearth and get to know the parts of me that had enabled me to survive the past. It was painful, scary and depressing, but I kept at it. Over time, I learned to trust her with the things I'd told no one else, and she helped me to learn to trust myself. This was a profound accomplishment for me. When I reached that level of trust, I felt I wanted to commemorate how far I'd come.

One day in a therapy session, I mentioned this desire to earmark my growth. I wanted to have something to remind me of how far I'd come. Something that would remind me of my accomplishments as I embarked on the pursuit of the fuller and more authentic expression of myself. I didn't know how to do that. She suggested I write a song. A song? I said, "Oh, okay. I think I can do that."

After some time and failed efforts, I came to realize I could not write a song. What to do? Google, of course! There are people who write songs for others. Of the ones that surfaced from my search, I was drawn to the website of Custom Crafted Songs. I liked what I read on the site about the founder. When I spoke with her, I knew I had found my songwriter, Anna Huckabee Tull. What had started as an unusual suggestion from my therapist turned into a full-scale, studio-recorded song.

About the collaboration from songwriter Anna Huckabee Tull:

To prepare for this song, Dawn and I talked for a good while. She was effusive about the many ways in which her therapist had taught her to more deeply understand and listen to herself, and to strengthen her own vision of what might be possible for her in her life. She shared openly with me, deeply as well, about many of the painful hurts from her past. You can't begin to know until you have walked a mile in my shoes how honored and astonished I feel when someone whom I have only just recently met feels close enough to me, through my music, to share from the deepest places within herself, their hurts and their joys.

I listened to Dawn's story and found myself in tears. Her story is private, but I can say this: I wish no child would ever have to go through what Dawn has gone through. And I wish that every child who has faced a childhood as painful and confusing as hers must have been could be as resourceful as she has been in stepping forward, finding help and learning to speak her own truths. As Dawn talked about her childhood, she shared that, in order to get through a lot of the pain back then, she used to "go away" within herself. And, suddenly, it hit me: perhaps her fears about abandonment now were traumatic for her precisely because of the way that, as a child, she taught herself to "go away." And, while it saved her life in a way, back then, those same coping mechanisms of "going away" might be causing her to abandon herself repeatedly, now, whenever she felt pain or discomfort. What would it sound like, we asked, if she was able to give a different message to herself, when she was hurting or in pain or afraid? And, thus, the song "Little Secret" was born.

Note: You can listen at:
https://www.customcraftedsongs.com/
uploads/1/5/8/9/15895028/littlesecret.mp3

LITTLE SECRET
By Anna Huckabee Tull

You let me in on a little secret
You kept telling it 'til I started to
Wonder if maybe someday I'd believe it
You said I deserve to open up
To love this life and feel love

And I believe it could be true
Because of all the things I'm learning when I'm
*   learning with you*

SHE HE ME

Who I have been for myself in moments when I
*   have been hurt*
And who I'm learning to be, for me

I am strong enough to share the way I feel
I am brave enough now to learn to let myself heal
And I am trusting enough to believe you when you say

I will not leave, I will not walk
I am right here believing in you, and I will not stop
I will not desert you or turn away
I am here for you, by your side and I will stay

So now I will let you in on a little secret
It's one you kept whispering and now
I see what it means when I dare to believe it
I do deserve to open up
To be here for myself and to feel that love

And now I see how that is true
How I can be here for me the way I learned to from you
And in those moments when I hurt
Now I can say to myself

I will not leave, I will not walk
I am right here believing in me, and I will not stop
I will not desert myself or turn away
I am here for me, and I will stay

(c) 2008 Anna Huckabee Tull

I shared the song with my therapist. She hadn't really understood, until then, the incredible role she played in my life. She couldn't know, from deep within my painful past, how she so profoundly helped me find an optimistic and resilient picture of possibility for my future.

I later discovered that she contacted Anna, the songwriter, with the letter below:

"I was extremely humbled, speechless, emotional and 'blown away' by the song. Dawn is one of the most incredible people I have worked with. She continues to move forward, fight, feel and believe in the process against all things (fear) that tell her, 'Don't do it!'"

So many people would have 'given up' long ago, considering the pain and trauma she has experienced in her life. I wish I could put into words what I feel when I sit with her, and hear her story, and feel her pain and look at her with disbelieving eyes, wondering how she has continued to strive for all these years. I feel humbled by her because she has chosen me. I sit in the room and listen, and I am let in on her secrets... that she has held for so long. That have crippled her...that she is finally letting go of...so that she can grow and become the beautiful woman that she is. Dawn has so much to give others."

I would have this, my song, one that spoke to my journey, my struggle, my heart, my future and the heart of the relationship that got me there.

I had finally connected to the undying spirit deep within me that allowed me to survive for so long and would support me from now on. As I began to love and stand up for myself, my world changed. The way I saw myself was different. I was different.

I saw a brighter vision of what my life could be. This song was my musical mantra. I could play it even in my head anytime I needed to. It would help me go forward to create the life I wanted. And, it could remind me I had the courage to live it.

If I wanted a new future, I had to know what my definition of happiness was, what a happy life could be. Quickly, and in no uncertain terms, I admitted to myself that being married to Terry, a man, was so wrong for me. I was tired of the charade and could not endure the anger and depression I was living with. I knew I was happiest when I was in a relationship with a woman. My therapy and the work I'd done there reaffirmed I was definitely not straight. I had to divorce Terry. After several painful phone calls, he agreed to my decision to divorce. We became legally separated.

COMES THE DAWN

Almost instantly, I felt relieved. Divorce was not a failure; it was an act of authentic kindness for both of us. Because Terry was on duty overseas, the process would take more time than if he were in the States.

I reclaimed my courage and my sexual orientation as lesbian and went back on Match.com—this time as a woman looking for a woman. I had little luck. My subscription was about to expire, and I decided I was going to delete my account after taking one final scroll through. Only one person interested me. I considered sending a "wink," but a direct message seemed wiser in that it was my last day online.

When the response came, we exchanged phone numbers. In a strange coincidence, we were both named Dawn with birthdays in June. A sign?

We texted for a while, and I learned that Dawn's Match.com subscription was also about to end. When we finally set a time to meet, we agreed it would be at my house. I instantly became anxious. What would I wear? How could I guess what the right thing would be? Just as anxiety was rising in me, I got the text message, "Can we agree on one thing? Can we please both wear jeans?" Hell YES! Another sign?

That evening, I waited on the porch outside in my best jeans and with sweaty palms.

I thought I saw the car pass the house, and I was right. The car turned around and parked and Dawn got out, approaching the stairs. All the while, my heart was pounding. We said, "Hello," and that was it. The connection with my dog was immediate, too. You can always trust your dog, and that IS a good sign.

We went to the movies. By the time the night ended, we both knew we'd found something special.

I learned that Dawn was in the process of separating from a long-term relationship and preferred the pronouns they/them. Of course, that was fine with me.

I was still married to Terry. I didn't keep the relationship with Dawn a secret from Terry; I let him know soon after our first meeting.

After a few dates, I knew I'd found what I had been looking for my whole life.

We've been together ever since. Living with Dawn was wonderful and frightening for me at the same time. It hasn't always been easy. It was my first new and real relationship after all I had learned in therapy. I was scared. I was unsure of what to expect from me and from the relationship. Would the anger I had always had with Terry still be a problem? Would I erupt? And, if I did, would I scare Dawn away?

I realized that the depth of my anger was so much more than just the residual from the marriage. It came to the surface in different ways for different reasons. I admit I was difficult, afraid of having a relationship and afraid of losing it. It made me confused, passive-aggressive, negative, moody and frequently pessimistic about the future. I was struggling. That was clear to Dawn. They voiced a dislike for my behavior and concerns for our relationship but remained steadfast, all the while reassuring me they would not leave me. What they said was they saw something beyond what was outwardly being shown to them. Somehow, they recognized that, underneath my angry exterior, there was a person they knew was there—the person they loved. They believed in me when I didn't believe in myself. What a gift.

It did not take long for my mom to see the difference my relationship with Dawn had on me. Even in her critical eyes, she could see I was better, happier. She liked Dawn, probably better than she liked me. The way she treated us as a couple, I could tell my mother recognized that my marriage to Terry was never right. I suspect she may have felt bad about that; we never discussed it.

Even though I was happier being with Dawn, something was still nagging at me. The struggle was still there daily. I'd finally found my true love, so why wasn't that enough? Shouldn't I be satisfied? I thought I could be, for everyone else's sake. I was openly lesbian and accepted by my mother. I was still not myself, but at least I was looking forward to the future for the first time.

I graduated from SCSU with a 3.7 GPA and a bachelor's degree. In September 2010, I enrolled in an accelerated one-year master's program in Social Work at Fordham University. I expected it to be intense, but I felt good about it. My life was finally coming together. Dawn and I were planning our future, which included saving money to buy the house with the white picket fence once I had my degree.

The white picket fence came sooner than expected. Sadly, it was the one at my mother's house. In October 2010, my mother was diagnosed with Alzheimer's disease. When the time came that she needed it, Dawn and I moved in with her as her caretakers.

MOM

I clearly remember the day we received her diagnosis. When the doctor said it was Alzheimer's, the anxiety and dread I always felt around my mother exploded into a million shards of emotional glass. Disbelief, anger, fear, resentment and anxiety sent waves of nausea rolling through my body. What am I supposed to do now? Am I supposed to step up and take care of her? What has she done to deserve my care? Would she do it for me? I couldn't believe she deserved to be cared for, especially by me. After all, she wasn't there for me when I needed her most. But I knew what would be expected of me. Isn't taking care of a sick mother the responsibility of the oldest daughter? I was THE daughter, so that let everyone else off the hook.

I struggled with what the responsibility of her care would mean to my life. No matter how angry and resentful I was, I knew she couldn't be on her own. No one else in the family would step up; they were all too self-absorbed.

My relationship with my mother was never easy. If I were to choose one word to describe it, it would be conflicted. She was always physically present and

46

yet distant. Birthdays, Christmas and school-related events were compulsory, but still felt disconnected.

On the outside, it may have appeared typical, but, below the surface, there was a strange discord. I did not live up to her expectations. I didn't want to.

I was always at fault. When I was being threatened or getting physically abused by other adult family members, she didn't come to my rescue. Instead, she would make me apologize to them as if I were responsible for their abhorrent actions. Even after exclaiming to her I did nothing wrong, she would say, "Just apologize."

Something kept her from loving me the way I longed to be loved by her, the way we expect a mother to love her child. I can't believe she didn't realize how hurtful that was. Did she? Maybe she didn't want to? Maybe she just couldn't. I don't know why. I don't know if something happened to her in her early life, but I know neither of us enjoyed our relationship. It was a bond of discord and denial. In her lack of acceptance of me, I often felt her disgust. As a kid, I thought it was my fault. As an adult, I still couldn't come to terms with it. There were secrets. There were questions never to be asked, and discussions that should have taken place. Now Alzheimer's was about to dissolve the opportunities, if there were any.

As with most battered children, I was ever dutiful and hopeful. Despite that trauma, I would never wish for a deadly disease to befall her… us. I couldn't let go of the fact that I loved her and the feeling that she could have done better by me.

I felt bad for her in that she'd just retired that very year. She'd worked hard all her life and had moved on after divorcing an abusive, cheating husband. She was an independent, stubborn 62-year-old woman. One of the hardest times in her illness was telling her she could no longer drive. The doctor had to intervene. Relinquishing her car keys was devastating for her.

In the early days of her illness, my mother fooled people. Relatives would look confused, challenging me with, "What are you talking about? She has Alzheimer's disease?"

For the first year, Dawn and I continued to live right next door in our own place. We checked on Mom frequently and had a monitoring system installed in her house so we could easily check on her throughout the day. Dawn changed their work schedule in order to work from home three days a week so they could be there to monitor and care for Mom.

When part-time care was no longer enough, Dawn and I took charge in making the renovations to her living space. We also renovated the basement to create separate living quarters for us, and we moved in.

We couldn't leave my mother alone. We did what we had to do, though it was extremely difficult for us. We had very little personal time or normalcy in our lives, with work, school and taking full-time care of her. We put our social life and own priorities on hold for three years.

It took me time and a lot of patience, which I didn't have, to adjust to Mom, or should I say the disease. It constantly annoyed me when she would ask the same question repeatedly. I couldn't hold back my annoyance, and there were some verbal lashings. Dawn saved me. They supported me while calmly caring for my mother, despite how my mother treated them. To this day, I do not know how Dawn did it. They could just go with the flow of whatever was happening. They are the most inspiring person I have ever met. I admire and love them so much. Taking a lesson or two from Dawn, I figured out what I needed to do to calm down and handle Mom and my stress. I found sanity in accepting what was happening and flowing with the tide of the situation as it shifted.

Early on, Dawn and I agreed to what our caregiving boundaries were. When my mother's care required more than we felt comfortable doing, we agreed we would have to find professional care for her. That came after three long years of caring for her at home. It was a tough decision, but it was time to move her to a nursing home facility. There was something so devastating about seeing how my mom had absolutely no control over anything in her life anymore. She was no longer the woman I knew; she was an empty shell of a woman who looked like my mother.

Of course, the ever-absent family members who were nowhere to be found during our three years of care were angry that we'd placed her in a home. They insisted she did not belong there. What did they know? How dare they?! I did what I believed was best for my mother and for us, too.

The nursing home was close by so I could visit her several times a week. This made visiting easy and gave me the physical and emotional separation I needed. The breathing room gave me a break and a new perspective. I came to realize my mother had done the best she could, in that she lived with my abusive father. He was a nightmare of a person and an angry and violent spouse. It was the first time that I could have compassion for her. I also realized how the disease must have made her feel—as helpless and as lost as I did during my entire childhood. There was only one way out of this horrid disease; nothing could fix it. All I could do was be there for her. Ironically, I became my mom's voice when she could not talk. I was the advocate for her I wished she'd been for me. There were days when she didn't know who I was, but still she seemed to be aware that she was safe with me and could feel that I really cared. For the first time in our relationship, we were in harmony.

After seven years of hell, she passed on June 30, 2017, with me and Dawn by her side. We lay next to her, holding her hands. The last thing she heard were our two voices saying, "Goodnight."

She was buried on her 70th birthday. The entire family came to the funeral, yet never once did they visit during her worst moments. They never saw her eyes filled with the shadow of death. Instead, they came to the funeral and cried their eyes out, as if her death was a surprise and changed their lives. When I placed the last flowers on her casket, I said my last, "Happy Birthday, Mom."

Even though I never felt she cared for me or protected me, I loved my mother. Even though she rejected who I was and didn't support me when I dared to tell her my most delicate secret, during her disease, I came to realize that nothing compares to losing your mother. She gave me life; she helped to make me who I am. From the day of her diagnosis, I grieved the loss of the years past. I grieved each aspect of her I lost as I witnessed her go through it. Her death left me with grief for words of acceptance and love I will never hear.

Even with all that was missing in our relationship, I loved my mother and always will.

Mom, even though you couldn't accept me for who I was, you still helped me grow up to make my own decisions. I miss you, Mom. I hope you are proud of the person I have become.

After her death, I added an Alzheimer's ribbon tattoo to the ones on my arm for her and for Caroline who had also succumbed to the disease.

MOVING FORWARD

During the seven years of my mother's struggle with Alzheimer's, I refused to let the important things in my life be compromised—my schooling, my career and my relationship with Dawn. They were so loving and accepting of me, it was getting easier to acknowledge who I really was. My ability to hide was becoming too much to suffer.

In a moment of sheer bravery, I asked Dawn if they would go shopping with me. They agreed. I had to qualify the request by adding, "I mean in the men's department."

The request didn't seem to faze them. Afterwards, they said I acted like a kid in a candy store. I was so excited; I couldn't hide my delight. It was a milestone for me, a day I look back to as the first step I took in embracing the masculinity I had been hiding for so long.

So began what I did not have the words for then, but now would say was my social transition. I got a man's style haircut, and from then on wore only men's clothing. I felt so much more empowered. This transpired in the earlier stages of my mom's disease, but she didn't seem to notice the change, or didn't question it.

I assumed she'd gotten used to my style of dress and didn't seem to notice a big difference.

Out in the world, I received mixed reactions. Some people addressed me as Miss or Ma'am, others as Sir. Being addressed as a female made me unhappy. I wondered, *Did my voice give me away? Was it the shape of my body?* Whatever it was, I did not like it. When addressed as a male, it angered me. At first, my own reaction surprised me until I realized that it was because I was not truly a male and wanted to be. It felt worse. When I talked to Dawn about it, they listened patiently and compassionately.

Dawn was so open, which allowed me to be open with them about wanting to do something about my breasts. I searched the internet and found the solution. Chest binders. They are the reverse of a bra, designed to flatten breasts. They looked interesting. It seemed like my solution. I read the description and studied the pictures that showed how they worked. When I saw the photos of the models in them and how they looked, I was sold! I ordered a few of them.

I could hardly contain myself when the package arrived. This was just what I needed to present myself as a guy! Finally, I had something that would help mitigate the feeling of dysphoria that breasts gave me.

How the hell do I put this on? It sure didn't look like it was going to fit. After a brief attempt, I yelled for Dawn. "I think I need your help!" They entered the bedroom to find me tangled, half in and half out of the binder. My neck and one arm were in the wrong holes. Everything was twisted, and I was sweating from the exertion. They laughed. I know it was intended to make me laugh and chill out. I was just too distressed and emotional.

They helped me out of my predicament and then back into the binder the correct way. I couldn't pull it down over my chest because it was all rolled up and stuck against my back. We tugged and pulled until it was in its prescribed position. Yikes! It was so damn tight. My thoughts went to what would happen later when it was time to take it off. How the hell am I going to do that by myself? Does this mean I can never do this by myself? While I loved having the help, it just wasn't practical.

The binder did flatten me quite a bit, but it wasn't very comfortable. The longer I kept it on, the more uncomfortable it became. As the day progressed, the compression of my entire chest hurt, and there were times it was painful to take a deep breath. Exercising in one was impossible, but the gymnastics I went through to get one on after a shower proved to be a workout in itself. I appreciated Dawn's attitude about it all and having the extra pair of hands to help.

With the difference in the way my chest looked with the binder, I felt more confident, which raised my self-esteem. I was more comfortable shopping in the men's department without attention.

After the initial thrill of my improved physical appearance waned, I became obsessed with imagining people could still tell I had breasts. I was not flat enough. People will laugh at me. Those thoughts fueled my insecurity all over again.

Once I had taken those first steps toward presenting as male, there was no turning back. This feeling of empowerment was new. I loved it. I loved how I felt, and with that my self-esteem started to rise. I began to feel comfortable with me. This was the first time I said out loud, "I like myself" and actually felt it.

I had fully acknowledged and put energy into beginning to live my life as a man. I hated my chest, and binding it was just not enough. It wasn't who I was or how I wanted to look. I felt like my breasts were still screaming in defiance of my identity. And, for that matter, I couldn't endure the anger and injustice that I still had to sit to pee.

This new tilt in my life poured over into my relationship with Dawn. Even though we were going strong, I was wary of how far we could take this change in me. I kept telling myself I needed to go slowly with making changes in transformation. I knew I could easily jump in with both feet, but I was afraid I might ultimately end up losing Dawn. Despite their support, I realized all of this had the potential to endanger our relationship. What if Dawn leaves me? If I am no longer the person they fell in love with, what then?

Regardless of what we discussed, they were steadfast in assuring me that, regardless of the outside, I was still the same person and always would be, right down to my soul, and I would be loved as such. I got braver and went so far as to suggest I might be transgender. I wanted them to agree. I felt it would help me commit. Their consistent response was always the same. "You are still the same person on the inside. You are who you are. Why do we need to fixate on a label?"

The love and support I had from Dawn seemed to be too good to be true. And, the more I thought about everything, I realized how wrong it was to allow society to decide who I was. That also pertained to our relationship. Why should it matter to anyone but us?

During this pivotal time, Dawn taught me to find humor in challenges. They encouraged me and then challenged me to shift my negativity. Each time a negative comment came out of my mouth, they would immediately prompt me to think of and affirm three positive ones. Boy, did that make me angry! That didn't matter to them. It worked. I learned how to shift my perspective. A great tool of self-control.

2011 was an important year for me. In January, my divorce from Terry was final. In May, I graduated from Fordham University with my masters in Social Work. My mom attended the ceremony. For the first time in my life, she told me she was proud of me.

I immediately began working as a therapist in Geriatric and Adult Psychiatry to satisfy the 3,000 hours of post-degree experience I was required to take in preparation for the exam to acquire my state license. The focus of the practice gave me experience with Alzheimer's disease, dementia, anxiety disorders and Geriatric Psychology.

Also, that December, Dawn and I were married. On our wedding day, we danced to "The Little Secret," the song Anna Huckabee Tull had written for me. Now it was for us.

HONESTY

Being married to Dawn was more than I ever thought I would find in a relationship. And, presenting as male was a huge milestone, but deep down I was still not totally happy with myself. I still hated my body and had actually discovered there was a term for what I was feeling about it—gender dysphoria—which is emotional distress caused by lack of congruence between gender identity and sex at birth.

I realized that I needed to go back to therapy. We were still taking care of my mother, and issues surrounding my work situation were unusually difficult. I needed to find the right therapist to work with me on those issues, though I knew I had much deeper problems that needed exploration. I sought out therapists, and when I found one who seemed right for me there were no openings. The person I spoke with on the phone referred me to someone else. I called and made an appointment.

At that first appointment, Tosh, the therapist, met me, a female. While I knew that was a lie, I struggled, wondering if I could tell my secret. Would it be weird to say I identify as male when I don't look or sound like a male? I was too afraid. Instead, we addressed the problems I presented about work, the stress of passing the state's licensure exam and family issues that were mostly about my mother's Alzheimer's disease and my resentment about being her caregiver. As desperate as I was to confess my secret to Tosh, it was too soon for me.

I did, however, begin to consider having breast reduction surgery. This was difficult to say out loud to anyone. I constantly wondered if the surgery would help answer the deep calling of the real me. Would it help me be me? Maybe the reduction would help me feel more comfortable in my body?

It took me a long time to actually verbalize my thoughts. Eventually, I got the courage to tell Dawn what I was thinking and feeling—that I longed to have the chest of a male. I was afraid of her reaction. Despite their support to that point, I was afraid they might leave me, that the result of the surgery would be something they couldn't endure. We discussed it for months and at great length. They said they would support whatever I chose. The choice was mine, but we were both unsure of exactly how I could vet my decision or go about finding a doctor under the circumstances.

During the process of making the decision, I repeatedly questioned whether I was making the right choice. What would it be like? Was it the right choice? Would it really make a difference in how I felt? Should I consider full breast removal instead?

Being cautious, I decided I could be satisfied with the less radical solution. I was apprehensive about the finality of a breast removal and chest reconstruction surgery. While I trusted Dawn's promise not to leave me, I wondered how either of us could really know how the change would affect each of us and our relationship.

I researched my options and searched for a plastic surgeon who would perform the surgery. When I finally committed to myself, I met with Dr. Reilly, a local plastic surgeon. I felt he was the right person for me. Finally, in November 2015, after 18 months of soul searching, I had the surgery. It went well; however, I quickly realized that I had made the decision from a place of fear. It wasn't enough. I wouldn't be happy without being rid of breasts altogether. I knew I wanted the surgery.

Once the breast reduction regret came over me, I absolutely knew I had to be true to myself or be miserable for the rest of my life. I was afraid. My breasts had to go. Again, what about my spouse? How would they feel if their spouse had no breasts? Every aspect of the decision and thoughts of life afterwards were fraught with the fear of losing them. How will they feel about me? What might it mean?

I didn't talk about this with Tosh. As we built trust, I began to wonder as I drove to each session if that would be the day to confess my secret. Disappointed in myself, I would leave without opening up about it. Perhaps next session? The hope of that helped to carry me to the next session, but it didn't happen.

It was around that point in time I also discovered the book, "Becoming Who I Was Always Meant to Be," by Chaz Bono, a transgender male. I felt as if the book was written for me. I never knew anyone like me. I didn't know there was anyone like me. Growing up I had only straight role models. No one to emulate or to help me understand what was going on with me.

There were so many things about Chaz's experience that deeply resonated with me. His thoughts and feelings were just like mine, right down to the breast reduction surgery. Chaz had done the same thing, a breast reduction, and realized, as I did, it wasn't enough. *I AM NOT ALONE.* For the first time in my entire life, I felt someone understood me. There is someone who knows. Someone who validates my feelings in this gender straightjacket I'd worn all my life.

I started talking about the book with my spouse, which helped me seize the opportunity to share things that stood out for me about what I'd read in it. Things that resonated with me—what it was like for me and how I felt. They listened compassionately and encouraged and supported me fully. Regardless of my choices, to them I would still be the person, heart and soul they fell in love with.

All of this gave me the safe space to talk more openly about getting chest reconstruction surgery. It was still complicated. As much as I wanted it, it brought up new fears. How prepared was I for this and what would follow? Would I embark on a total medical transition? What I'd done to this point wasn't final. This decision was both exciting and frightening—totally life-altering. How Dawn felt about it, about and who I would become was important. We talked extensively about all the possibilities, pros and cons. The surgery would make my body more congruent with the inner me. This was a commitment to so much more than surgery. It was fundamental to my journey to claim my real identity. I believed it was the answer. Was I right? Dawn lovingly encouraged me to pursue and embrace my male gender identity.

While I had to wait to heal from my breast reduction surgery to go forward with more surgery, I started to plan.

I was still in therapy with Tosh, and we reached a point at which it became clear it was time to conclude the therapy relationship. They pointed out that we'd worked on all the problems I had come to address. I wasn't surprised but I was devastated. I drove away from the office with tears streaming. I was sad and angry with my cowardice. I'd failed to allow myself to get the help I longed for. I pulled off the highway, stopped the car and thought, *It's now or never*! *What are you going to do?* I grabbed my cell phone and called Tosh before I chickened out. "I've been holding back on talking about some things in therapy. Can I come back next week? I need to talk."

I was relieved and scared to hear "Yes." The terrible weight was lifted, and on its heels came the Holy Shit moment. I knew that I'd opened Pandora's Box. And, as the story goes, there was no stuffing the secret back in. One phone call broke the long-suffered barrier between sharing the imposter me and the real me with someone else besides Dawn. It was a turning point in being honest about who I really was. That was scary. As daunting as breast reduction surgery was, this was actually the beginning of "baring my chest" to the world.

There are no coincidences. It turned out that Tosh's specialty was counseling the transgender community!

Therapy with Tosh help me continue the conversation with Dawn. We talked about gender and the fluidity of gender. I was finally able to express that I felt I was truly male on the gender spectrum. We delved deeply into ongoing discussions about the possibilities of me transitioning, exploring what that would mean for me and for us as a couple.

Dawn continued to stand by me with each new step I took in planning a path and finally making the life-altering decision. The plan held the future of me in such a dramatic way, changing my body so drastically. I was making a plan to birth a new future, birth me. I thought about what I needed to make that happen. Trust and support were at the top of my list. I had Dawn, and I thought of Dr. Reilly. I knew I wanted him with me on this journey to me. The journey to uncover the man I knew I was inside.

THE PLAN

My first commitment to the plan came in August that year. Until this point, everything I'd done had been a compromise. I'd been silently sitting on the gender fence by dressing in masculine attire and claiming to be lesbian. Presenting myself as such was something a majority of the general public seemed to accept.

I thought a logical next step would be to legally change my name. While this marked the first step and a personal triumph, like every other step to this point, it was difficult. Unlike other steps, though, this one was not about the judgment of the scrutiny of the outside world. It was difficult for me. It was more difficult than I could have ever have imagined.

What's in a name? I hadn't given that any thought. For 45 years, I had answered to my birth name, Dawn. I had not considered how ingrained it was, and how I'd not given a thought to how responding to the name was so automatic.

While the name may not have been indicative of how I wanted to be identified, it was my name. Me. It was then that I fully realized how names are more than an identifier to the world. I considered all of the legal ramifications, but I'd not given any thought to the difficulty of my own emotional and practical adjustment to offering myself as "Dayne." It wasn't natural. It was challenging. I had to catch myself every time I introduced myself. Any time I was asked for my name, Dawn came to my lips. I had to learn to pause before I answered to catch up with myself. I also had to train myself not to respond to the name Dawn when I heard it. The fact that Dawn was my spouse's name complicated things for me! God certainly has a sense of humor!

This transition from Dawn to Dayne was a very pivotal moment, the first of many changes I wanted to make. It was not only the transition of my gender; it was the decision to finally put myself first, regardless of the wishes, rules and scrutiny of others. I had always put everyone else's feelings before my own so as not to anger, disappoint or embarrass them. Everyone's opinions carried more weight with me than my own. Before coming out as transgender, I was constantly worried about what everyone else would think about me—about my appearance, my behavior and my life-style. All of that had to take a backseat or be thrown out the window. I would not be able to go on. It felt like it was a choice between life and death for me.

I needed to live my life as the authentic me. While it might sound like I just stopped worrying and caring about what others thought, it was more the culmination of a lifetime of self-denial. I knew I had to finally live my life authentically. I could no longer live a lie to make other people feel more comfortable. I had built the courage and faith in myself. It was my life. With the amazing support from my spouse. It was time for Dayne to come home. Transgender male.

Still, I knew I would have to face every one of the "what ifs" I'd considered before I made the decision to transition. What if I lose my job? What if the friends who had become my family of choice reject me, abandon me? What if Dawn is wrong about how they would see the new me and feel about me? What if my therapy clients lose confidence in me and quit? What if my clients don't accept a transgender therapist? How will I be shamed when people find out? How will I withstand the scrutiny? What embarrassment will I have to endure, and how will I manage?

I knew as I discussed my medical transition with Dawn I would have to do all I could to reassure them, and do all I could to make them comfortable with my choice. We talked about every detail of the surgery. More than breast tissue removal, it would involve contouring my chest to be more masculine looking. I would have scarring, which I was fine with, but how would that be for them? The surgery would take away the nipple sensation. I tried to anticipate what their concerns would be, and, when I did, I was wrong. I learned to listen carefully to their concerns and worried more about them than I did about me. Yes, it would be painful, but I would be getting what I wanted. Did they realize what *they'd* be getting? Would they ultimately be okay?

My therapy sessions with Tosh helped me through so much of the emotional process and were as instrumental in the support of my decision as Dawn was. It was during this time I came to realize I'd discovered a new professional calling. My lifelong experiences and this process made me realize I wanted to work with the LGBTQ+ community. I felt the compassion and passion to be the confidant, support and guide that Tosh had been for me. I wanted to offer the same to clients. I wanted to help the people I served find the path to being true to themselves, the way Tosh had helped me.

I'd just passed my LCSW State Licensure exam and, with that, went the concerns I'd had about losing my job because of my transition. Having my license meant I could and would go into private practice. I'd be my own boss. I certainly wasn't going to fire myself for being transgender! In fact, it could allow me to specialize in gender-related counseling if I so desired.

Despite what I saw for my future, when I opened my private practice, I did not have the community of clients in that niche specialty as I might have I wanted. However, there is such a thing as serendipity. The therapy practice I was connected with was relocating to Maryland. They approached me to see if I would be interested in taking over their group of transgender adult clients. It was the perfect entre into specializing in the work I desired. I agreed and began attending trainings and seeking out consultants who had the experience I could learn from.

* * *

In April of 2017, I attended a Transgender Lives Conference in Connecticut. I was enriching my professional knowledge, connecting with resources for my clients and looking for resources for my own transition.

At the conference, I introduced myself to Katherine Tierney, APRN, a practitioner who had expertise in

LGBTQ Health and Transgender Hormone Therapy. I'd referred clients to her but had never actually met her. This time, I asked if I could make an appointment to discuss my own hormone therapy.

My appointment the following Monday filled me with empowerment and excitement for a bright future. What I was embarking on would take a team of professionals, and I was assembling my team.

My first appointment with Katherine Tierney was to understand the details of my Hormone Replacement Therapy (HRT). She told me what I might experience from the therapy and what bodily changes I would most likely experience. Blood work was required before I could make a follow-up appointment.

I was filled to the brim with excitement and happiness. Then, just as strongly, anxiety and fear kicked in. The HRT meant I would be injecting myself with testosterone once a week. I hated needles. Even though I have many tattoos, this was different.

THE EXECUTION

A few weeks later, it began. Katherine explained everything again. I had my first shot, and I was on my way! I felt AMAZING. I'd taken control of my life, the life I wanted. No one could stop me now.

I knew there are many people with varied medical reasons who need to inject themselves. But, as hard as I tried, I couldn't do it. I could not give myself a weekly testosterone injection. Thanks again to Dawn, they did it for me every week for two years. After that, I switched from testosterone injections to daily androgen gel applications. It turned out that getting the injection was very anxiety provoking for me. Later, through the course of my working with other transgender individuals, I discovered I was not the only one. Many transgender men have injection anxiety. Often, it causes these patients to delay the injection, and inconsistent injections are not good protocol.

Regardless of what I was told, in my mind, I expected that by the time three months had passed I would be seeing signs of facial hair. Not the case! Every day I inspected my appearance looking for changes. I was always disappointed. I didn't anticipate how long it would take. That became more discouraging than I had expected.

I learned that transition does not work that way. I guess a parallel example is puberty. Those changes don't happen in a few months either. It definitely took time for the changes to show up, and, when they did, wow! There were many physical, mental and emotional changes.

I realized I was going through what I call Puberty 2.0. It was as difficult as the 1.0 experience was and about as much fun. Each one surprised me. To begin with... acne! I thought those days were behind me. It came back this time with a vengeance, even on my chest and my back. It lasted about a year, and it was so extreme I had to see a dermatologist for medication.

Then there was a change in body odor. I smelled different. The scent changed and got stronger for sure. My urine smelled different, too!

I experienced hair loss on my head and ended up with the balding patterns I saw in my family. Yet, hair was growing everywhere else on my body.

The skin on my face felt rougher. However, my facial hair wasn't growing as much as I'd wanted and expected.

My appetite changed. I was hungrier, and I gained weight because of it. Of course, my clothes didn't fit, and my feet grew one size larger. My voice started crackling, starting with a kind of sore throat-type scratchy tone. Then it deepened to sound as if I had a cold. I even had a lot of joint pain.

I think the emotional mood swings were more unexpected than the others. I became irritated, frustrated and angry more often and more easily. There were times when Dawn responded to my outbursts with a *this is what I was afraid of* look. The most surprising change in my emotional responses was that I stopped crying. Not totally, but certainly it was reduced to about ninety-five percent of what I'd experienced in my pre-transition life.

Not least of all was my sex drive! It went through the roof. I discovered why teenage boys take forever in the shower and why they showered often. Over time, it became annoying. Before I could concentrate or do almost anything, I had to get relief. I kept thinking, I am too old for this!

But, it was all worth it.

Once I got past Puberty 2.0, I felt more confident and much better about myself. It took about eighteen months, but I began being addressed as Sir and referred to as he/him. It felt weird to hear it, much like getting used to my name change. The days of being addressed as "ma'am" were all but gone. If it did happen, I was thrown into instant despair, mostly because it crushed my new identity. I just pretended not to hear the person. Still, it affected my confidence and made me doubt my own identity for a while, until I could shake it off.

Chest masculinization surgery was the next step in my transition. As far back as I can remember, having breasts was like having alien objects attached to my chest. I hated them and avoided mirrors because of it. Getting dressed every day was emotional agony. I struggled with my appearance and my ability to silence the anger and self-critical voices in my head. The worst part is that the feeling was always with me, but it became layered with fear when there were social events with dress codes, like the beach or weddings.

SHE HE ME

Unlike the typical female, I prayed that I would get breast cancer so I could have them removed. It probably sounds awful to welcome major surgery willingly to remove parts of your body. After all, it isn't lifesaving in the medical sense, yet in a different way it was for me. For women who do undergo full mastectomies for lifesaving reasons, perhaps they share some of the feelings I had. Perhaps the loss of breasts that are a natural part of you and your identity comes the closest to how I felt having them. While others cannot always tell about you by your physicality, for you and your spirit, it's always there underneath it all. I have great compassion for the fear, anxiety and depression these women must feel. For me, though, the surgery would be the end to those exact feelings. Sadly, one cannot gift their breasts, or I would have.

It had become so clear, after my breast reduction, that removing them entirely was what I wanted and needed. I felt certain it would rectify my gender dysphoria. I knew that not only would surgery increase my external and internal sense of self, it would inevitability bolster my confidence and self-esteem. Like many trans-identified men, it was crucial for my well-being and quality of life.

I thought about my breast reduction surgery with Dr. Reilly, and I knew I wanted him to be part of the team I would need to make my transition. I made the appointment to see him about completing what we had started. When surgery day came, I was prepared and so ready. The apprehension over having major surgery was minor compared to the joyous anticipation of becoming the long-awaited version of me.

71

To my surprise, I was able to go home the day of surgery. For the next several days, I needed help with everything I did. Dawn was amazing. The pain was not horrible, but I did feel like I was run over by a truck, an eighteen-wheeler. The drains on both sides of my body were the worst part. They served to eliminate fluid buildup under the skin, which was essential for healing. They needed to be emptied several times a day, and Dawn was always there for me. Two weeks later they were removed. It wasn't as painful as I had imagined it would be. Once free of them, I was able to do more, and day-by-day I began to feel better, back to my new self.

I did have to wear a binder around my chest for two weeks and keep the incision areas clean and covered. My chest was flat! The incisions continued to heal with the expected scarring.

It's been three years, and I still have little to no feeling on most of my chest. Strangely, I can sometimes feel as if I have on a binder. For me, sometimes the feeling is so real, I actually have to feel my chest to check. I did some research to discover that there is a condition called Phantom Breast Syndrome that some mastectomy patients experience. There is a variety of associated sensations.

TRIUMPH

LIFE AS A MAN

In October of 2017, I took the final legal act of my transition—to change the gender classification on my birth certificate. It was profound, but not nearly as difficult to acquire as I had thought.

The process in Connecticut required a letter from a physician, advanced practice registered nurse or psychologist stating that you have "undergone surgical, hormonal or other treatment clinically appropriate for the applicant for the purpose of gender transition." However, "No particular procedure is required, and it is not necessary to list surgeries or medical procedures that have been undertaken."

The most liberating section of the form and the process was this small but powerful paragraph, a signed affidavit:

> "I, Dayne Bachmann, under the pains and penalties of perjury, declare that I have undergone appropriate treatment for the purpose of gender transition based on contemporary clinical standards, and that I am no longer the gender recorded

on my current birth certificate. I am therefore requesting that the gender marker on my birth certificate be changed from Female to Male."

Several years have passed since then. Recently, I saw a picture of myself in which I was holding my cell phone. For the first time, when I looked at it I saw a man's hands. Mine! Talk about excitement! I texted my spouse the picture and said, "Finally!" They laughed and agreed that they noticed that, too.

With all that it has taken to get to here, to this point in my life, I still have doubts. I am continually questioning myself— *Do I look like a man? Do I act like a man? Do people secretly question my gender?* Some of the doubt comes from what I am trying to understand about what it means to be a man in our society.

I often feel insecure about my behavior. I am not always sure how to conduct myself as a man. Sometimes I feel like I still have some feminine qualities. I sometimes think I am too sensitive or emotional, and I question if that's acceptable. If I am more passive than aggressive, can I still be a man? Can I enjoy the Hallmark channel and not be interested in basketball games? Is it okay to still like that my shoes and baseball cap match or that I like to spend more than a few seconds on my hair? What if I want to wear nail polish? Are all these things just the way I am, or are they conditioning?

What characteristics make someone manly? I study other men and take cues from watching how they behave. Sometimes, if I am in a situation in which I am unsure, I will ask one of my male friends if my clothing is okay or if they have advice about shaving.

Fortunately, I have acquired some really great friends who support me and don't make me feel embarrassed.

I know for sure from my own experience that men and women are quite different. I think that much can be learned by our society from the transgender community, who can offer so much insight from having lived life from both perspectives. Just ask my spouse!

Clearly, our society has many different rules for men and women. When I was a woman, if I wanted to console someone who was upset or crying, I would think nothing of comforting them with not only kind words, but some physical gesture, perhaps a hand on their shoulder or a hug. In our culture, men do not always have the freedom to respond that way. I had to be aware, evaluate the situation and gauge my reactions. I needed to learn to think before I acted and choose my outward behavior appropriately.

I learned to use caution before touching another person. I realize that my hand on someone's arm or shoulder as a gesture of comfort or compassion can be misconstrued, even considered a form of sexual harassment having legal repercussions.

On the flipside of the male/female cautions, the female programming that still remains in me makes me apprehensive about walking alone at night in an unlit parking lot. I don't think guys typically give it a thought. They are not taught to be as wary of the same situations as females. Of course, it is always smart to be aware of your surroundings, but I think it occurs to me more than most males.

Throughout my entire transition, one huge concern I had was unique to me. I feared that becoming a man might mean I would end up looking like my father.

Perhaps, with that, though I couldn't imagine it, there was the slightest fear that if I looked like him I would behave like him. I was afraid that, once I started testosterone, I would become abusive and a womanizer. I knew that didn't make rational sense, but childhood trauma creates irrational fears in us. Sometimes, when I look at myself in the mirror, I do see my father. I look just like him now. I *look* like him, but I am not *like* him, at all.

What I know for myself and from what I have learned from my clients, the transgender fear of using public restrooms is real. The restroom is one of the most threatening places for transgender individuals. Everyone has the need for the restroom, yet transgender people live in fear of that biological need in public places. The issue has garnered the public's fear and attention, and some states are requiring and challenging policy-making and laws.

Despite this overwhelming fear, I started using the men's room the day I started hormone therapy. It was a silent but defining decision indicating my commitment and acceptance of myself and my new life. There would be no going back. At the time, I didn't pass as male. I was filled with anxiety and fear, but I did it. I just kept my head down and got in and out quickly.

To this day, I still have anxiety using the men's room, as do other transgender people. We have to fight the feeling that we don't belong there. We fear for our safety should the wrong person discover us. That fear never dissipates. The danger comes from the anger and fear of those who would rather not even try to understand. I hope someday that will change.

When I am out with male friends, I always ask them if there were stalls in the restroom. Privacy. As many times as I ask and get the same answer, I still ask. I don't know if society will ever understand. I am grateful that I have not been outed, threatened, violated or physically harmed. That fear is always there. If my anxiety is too high, debilitating, I look for a family restroom.

Gym locker rooms are the same way. The possibility for exposure is even greater. So is the fear. The first time I walked into the gym locker room, the lights, the mirrors, one way to the showers, one way to the stalls and urinals, OVER STIMULATION. Not good for a guy who already has anxiety. I can't think or remember how to get from one section to the other. I get all mixed up navigating and can end up walking into naked men. So, besides not enjoying the gym for the purpose of exercising, I have locker room anxiety, too. Two strikes for the gym.

I don't know why, but when I think about men, of *being* a man, I instantly think "beard." Even though I've started to see some growth of my facial hair, a semblance of a patchy beard, I really desire a full beard. The laser hair removal I coveted in my early years was working against me now. I was told before starting hormone therapy that, because of my earlier hair removal, I might not be able to grow a beard. Too cruel. How I regretted the laser hair removal I'd had done on my face in my earlier years. I couldn't have known then that I would end up here, longing for even more than I had then when I was bullied as a female for having too much. Back then, it devastated my self-esteem, and now not having it does.

To see what might be possible, I found Dr. Bowden, a hair transplant surgeon in Connecticut. We discussed a beard transplant. I felt Dr. Bowden really understood me and the importance having a beard held for me. I was desperate to achieve this manifestation of my masculinity. He said he understood what a beard reflected in the male gender identity, and especially for me it could be even more psychologically important. For me it was twofold, the psychological, but also because I felt that having a beard would eliminate my being mis-gendered once and for all.

Before he would perform any surgery on me, Dr. Bowden had me try many non-surgical treatments with facial creams and such. Nothing worked; though it might for others, surgery was my only option.

During the time I was waiting for my beard transplant surgery, I came across a book written by Jeremy L. Wallace, *Taking the Scenic Route to Manhood*. He wrote: "I don't regret the next decision I made. Even though I couldn't afford to have surgery, I had saved up some money and decided to use a bit of it to have a facial hair transplant."

This was the first I had ever heard of another transgender male getting a beard transplant. Until that moment, I really thought I was the only one! I was so excited and relieved that I actually emailed Jeremy to see if he would consider talking with me. He agreed, and, when we met virtually, he answered my questions and put my mind at ease. And, yes, he was sporting an awesome beard!

In April 2021, I finally had the surgery. It involved transplanting somewhere in the range of twenty-one hundred hair follicles, harvested from the back of my head and transplanted on my face. I had no concern about the choice to have the procedure, only anxiety about the level of pain I would experience afterwards. It turns out it was an eight-hour process. It wasn't an easy day, but I was well cared for throughout.

Of course, I worried a bit about how it would actually look when healed. Would it be what I hoped for? Other than that, there was only a small shadow of sadness because my late grandfather would not be able to teach me how to shave.

The recuperation at home was a series of stages. I went from numb to discomfort to out-of-my-mind itchy. I thought about what I remember of an episode of the TV show "Friends." Phoebe and her boyfriend get chicken pox, and Monica wrapped their hands in oven mitts so they couldn't scratch. Dawn is my real-life Monica, but we left the oven mitts in the kitchen. Instead, I tried meditation and breathwork, both with varying success.

The beard is coming in nicely, and I am so pleased. It is a definite boost for my self-esteem, which has made my confidence rise. This was the last part of my transition. It helped me feel complete and whole. I can still get surprised and excited when I look in the mirror, and I am happy to say I have learned to shave because I have to!

This was the last part of my transition. It helped knowing I was going to feel complete in a few short months.

Feeling complete in your transition is different for everyone. And, as you will discover in the following pages, not every transgender person transitions the same way. For me, I knew going into my transition that

I wanted my voice to sound like a male, and hormone therapy took care of that. I knew that having "top surgery"—breast removal and chest reconstruction surgery—was a necessity in order for me to alleviate my dysphoria. Finally, I knew that having facial hair was a must for me, and with that I seemed to notice facial hair on men, even the ones on television! That ended when I finally had my own.

I am truly happy and content with the changes in my body, my appearance and my life as a result of my transition. What I realize now is that when my mother continually told me I needed a man in my life, I was now the man I needed all along.

REFLECTIONS

I mentioned at the beginning of the book that I didn't remember much of my childhood. What I want to share here is that I discovered much later in life how much was missing from my memory and, even later than that, what it actually meant.

One day, before my mother became ill, she pulled out a photo album from the 1970s. The pages had yellowed, and some of the photos had faded. As we sat together at the kitchen table, she turned the pages, stopping here and there to reminisce. She would point to a photo of me taken in some happy childhood setting or event and remark, "Oh! Remember this, or remember that time when…?"

I would think about it, trying hard to remember the day or even a moment of it, and, inevitably, I'd have to say, "Um no. No, I don't remember that."

"How could you not remember that?!" she'd exclaim.

Right, I thought, *how could I NOT remember, especially something that sounds like it would have been so much fun?*

Still, she continued pointing to pictures of a young me, hoping to spark my memory. In one photo, I was dressed up in a pink poodle recital outfit. *Dancing school?* Again I puzzled, *How do I not remember this? The outfit looks itchy and downright uncomfortable. Should I not at least remember that?*

Nearly all of the photos were of me wearing dresses with long luscious hair wrapped in a neatly bound ponytail. From my perspective, the girl in the photos could easily have been someone else, or perhaps a now-missing twin with whom I did not share the same experiences. I thought to myself, *Good God, what does this mean?* Why I would decide to throw these memories away and leave behind nothing but a black space of emptiness? Clearly, the photos represented real events in which I participated. I was physically there, but not mentally, it seems. This immense disconnect was a huge and frightening discovery for me.

Now, as a therapist, I know that sometimes we purposefully block out memories for our own emotional well-being. This can happen with PTSD. It's called Dissociative Amnesia, which occurs when a person blocks out certain times associated with a stressful or traumatic event. It turns out I had many! While I knew this at some level, which I have written about, becoming aware of the extent of the memory loss validates that my dysphoria, the experiences of childhood and my family's abusive behavior were a form of traumatic stress for me. Identifying that for myself helps me realize and be proud of how much I have survived just to be where I am today. I think that kind of validation is important, regardless of how long ago it happened. I offer this in consideration for anyone who experiences it, regardless of why whatever caused it is important to explore.

82

There were other types of validation for me that showed up more recently in my adulthood. It was not long after my mother passed. I happened to run into the parents of some of my former schoolmates, one of whom I was still an in contact with. They were aware of my gender presentation.

We were at a local diner, and I stopped at their table to say hello. The conversation got around to my mother's recent death. Often, after someone passes, people feel freer to share their memories and reflections. The two women commented about how difficult my mother had had it, in both being married to my father and in her life after the divorce. "She endured a lot with your father's behavior and treatment. You know, with your father's issues with mental illness and all."

Oh, my God, I thought. *I didn't imagine it. It wasn't me. It wasn't my fault.* This was the first time anyone had verbalized to me anything about my family's behavior.

With that, I walked away with a validation that opened the door to a new type of healing and relief. That kind of relief and release doesn't happen overnight, because our formative years with our families have an indelible influence on our lives. Getting validation of our experience from others helps.

I'd already learned that we don't get to choose our families or relatives, but we can learn from them. When we become independent, we get to make choices about relationships and who we need in our lives to support us. My family never fit those criteria for me. It turns out that there was good cause for that, and it wasn't me or related to my gender issues. Still, at the time, I chose not to have relationships with them. Any therapist will tell you that isn't easy.

More recently, the subject of my middle name came up in a conversation with a colleague whom I consider a friend. I chose to take my grandparent's last name, Romano, as my new middle name. She asked if I was related to another Romano, a female. I said, "Yes, she was married to my uncle Frank." It turns out my friend knew Frank and this wife of his (he'd had three). She said at the time she was acquainted with them and that she and her boyfriend would, on occasion, get an evening phone call from Frank's wife who was panicked because Frank was drunk again and waving his gun around. The rest of their evening was inevitably spent calming Frank down.

When I heard her story, I was saddened. What a horrible phone call to get and what an awful and possibly dangerous position to be put in. But, again, this was validation that it really wasn't me. It was nothing I'd done; it was Frank.

While I wish my upbringing had been different, I can also recognize how my family's critical and abusive behavior shaped my desire to be kind and inclusive of others. From there, I learned what good relationships are and how to have them. And I do.

Part of my teenage story was the desire to end my life. Today, we know that suicide among teens in our society has escalated for reasons we don't really understand. The point is the pain that leads to it is varied and serious. As a therapist, I fervently want to offer this: if a person plans their own death by suicide, they are desperate. Please consider this: first, you MUST realize you don't really want to die; you want the pain to stop. Get help. Second, don't give up five minutes before the miracle. Yes, miracles happen and are just around the corner. Third, when things are so bad you are at the end of your rope, tie a knot at the end of it and hold on (because things change).

BEING TRANSGENDER AND A THERAPIST FOR THE LGBTQ+ COMMUNITY.

I have noticed that people who suffer tragedy or major challenges in life often choose to become involved in some aspect of advocating or helping others who are having similar experiences.

I have always had the aptitude and desire to help others. It is how I ended up working in nursing homes in my early adult years. It is why I chose to become a therapist, and more specifically to help others who find themselves questioning gender norms.

My clients don't have to teach me about being transgender. I can understand what my clients are saying. I don't have to wonder what they mean when they talk about feeling that they were born in the wrong body.

Since clients need a therapist's letter of referral for hormone therapy or surgery, finding the right therapist is important. That person must serve as more than a "gatekeeper" to the next step.

Talk therapy can be of such great value with the right therapist. One does not have to have had the personal experience, but training and expertise is important. I believe working with the transgender community takes a special kind of training. That training is available to all therapists. And, clients all have the right to ask about the therapist's expertise, training and experience before they book an appointment.

Clients recognize they are in the right place when they walk in the door of my practice. They enter a waiting room that conveys acceptance, including a gender-neutral restroom. I have been told on so many occasions how comfortable and safe my transgender clients feel when coming to my office for the first time.

It is clear that the parents of young gender-questioning clients play a huge role in the process for their child. These parents have their own challenges, and I am continually awed by parents who create strong support systems for their children. Having not had the support I would have wanted, it pleases me to see these families successfully navigate the challenging choices and transitions of loved ones. I hope my story and my work will help to make the choice of authenticity easier for all.

INFORMATION AND RESOURCES

There is not just one way to be transgender. Understanding the terminology, complexity, questioning, transitioning and support of the transgender community can be confusing, even for those who are part of the community. The following information is intended to be a brief resource. Other resources can be found online, and some organizations' websites are listed at the end of this section.

HOW DO TRANSGENDER PEOPLE TRANSITION?

Not all transgender people undergo any physical transition. Transition can involve just social transition and/or medical transition. See below.

Social transitioning may include:

- Coming out to friends and family
- Asking people to use your desired pronouns (she/her, he/him, they/them)
- Adopting a name different from your birth name
- Changes in clothing that are aligned with gender identity
- Cutting hair short or growing it long
- Body language, mannerisms, posture
- Use of makeup, jewelry and accessories
- Non-permanent changes in appearance
- Use of binders or breast forms to change the appearance of the chest
- Use of packers or tucking to change genital appearance

MEDICAL TRANSITION MAY INCLUDE:

Transgender Youth

- Puberty Blockers - "pause button" for trans youth. Can prevent them from entering puberty in the wrong gender. The appropriate time to begin blockers is typically between the ages of 9 and 11 (tanner stage 2).

- Hormone Therapy - (HRT) Most providers in the U.S. start around the age of 16. Clients must be educated on the permanent changes, impact on fertility and risks of treatment.

Transgender Men

Medical transition *MAY* include any of the following:

- <u>Hormone therapy:</u> testosterone injection, androgen (gel), patches. Testopel is an implantable testosterone, and you can also do compounded cream (creates masculine characteristics, such as a deeper voice, facial hair growth, muscle growth, redistribution of body fat away from hips and breasts, cessation of periods, etc.)

- <u>Chest Masculinization surgery</u>, or "<u>top surgery</u>" - **double incision procedure:** A person who has this surgery tends to have larger breasts. This procedure entails two incisions below each breast, the breast tissue removed, and then the skin from top of the breast is pulled down flat and stitched to the incision. The nipples are removed and then grafted back on in the correct position. With this surgery, the person will not have sensation in their nipples. Recovery time for this procedure is approximately two weeks, and this can vary depending on the type of job and lifestyle you have—sedentary or physically demanding.

  Keyhole procedure is one in which an incision is made around the nipple area, and liposuction is performed to remove breast tissue. This procedure will minimize the scar you will have just around the outside of the areola. This type of surgery leaves the sensation intact. Recovery time for this procedure is approximately two weeks, which can vary depending on the whether you have a sedentary or physically demanding job and lifestyle.

- <u>Hysterectomy</u> - removal of uterus

- <u>Oophorectomy</u> - removal of ovaries

- <u>Phalloplasty</u> - this surgery will create a full-size penis. This surgery is complex, expensive and higher risk for complications. At the end, you may not have the desired look you thought you would have. The phallus is created with skin taken from your forearm, back or thigh as well as the nerves. Once you are healed, a penile implant can be put in so an erection can be achieved. This is the same implant used for men with erectile dysfunction.

- <u>Metoidioplasty</u> - release of the clitoris. The surgeon lengthens the urethra and repositions it so urine will expel from the end instead of underneath. With this surgery, the patient will be able to stand to pee. Also, with this procedure, a full hysterectomy will be performed, and the vagina will be surgically closed. The result of this will be having a small penis. At this time, a scrotoplasty, which is where a physician surgically creates a scrotum from the labial skin, is offered as an option. At this time, testicular implants can be added, but it is not necessary.

- <u>Pre-meta or clitoral release</u> is where the surrounding skin of the clitoris is removed, and the ligament is released from the pubic bone. This procedure will result in the clitoris being erect when excited. This does not grant the ability to stand when peeing.

*Not all transgender men decide to have these surgeries. There is no one way to transition.

TRANSGENDER WOMEN

Medical transition *MAY* include any of the following:

Hormone therapy involves spironolactone, which blocks testosterone, followed by estrogen treatment, which will induce physical changes to make the body more feminine. The two medications together can lead to breast growth, decreased body hair, redistribution of body fat and softening of the skin.

- Orchiectomy is a procedure in which one or more testicles are removed.

- Vaginoplasty is a procedure in which male genitalia are reconstructed into female genitalia (vagina/labia/clitoris).

- Breast augmentation is a procedure to increase breast size.

- Facial feminization is a surgery to change masculine features into feminine features, e.g., hairline can be moved to create a smaller forehead, lip and cheekbone augmented, jaw and chin reshaping and resized, face lift, etc.

- Hair transplant is a procedure in which hair follicles from one part of the body (donor site) are transferred to the site where a person would like more hair growth (recipient site).

*Not all transgender women decide to have these surgeries. There is no one way to transition.

Insurance companies follow WPATH guidelines: standards of Care (SOC) for the Health of Transsexual, Transgender, and Gender Nonconforming People.

https://www.wpath.org/publications/soc

Legal Options in Transition:

Change of name (legal name change involves a $225 filing fee at Probate Court).

Change of gender marker – Connecticut does not require surgery for a gender marker change. A medical doctor or Licensed Mental Health provider must sign a form from the DMV.

Birth Certificates in Connecticut require a medical doctor or psychiatrist to sign the form.

Passports - The State Department announced that passport applicants can now select their own gender marker: male or female. This means that transgender individuals who are traveling will no longer need to provide medical certification if their gender identity doesn't match the marker on their birth certificate or other documents. https://transequality.org/know-your-rights/passports.

BARRIERS IN SEEKING MEDICAL CARE:

1. Lack of education and awareness among providers

2. Physicians looking for the patient/client to provide education

3. Stigma

4. Significant increase in gender dysphoria when having to be seen by the OB/GYN or urologist

5. Identification complications. What you can do: listen to how patients refer to themselves and loved ones (pronouns, names) and use the same language they use. If you're unsure, ask.

THINGS THAT LGBTQ+ PATIENTS WISH PRACTITIONERS KNEW:

1. They come to you with an extra layer of anxiety.

2. They may have been verbally or physically abused (within the medical community).

3. Often, they experience discrimination within the health care setting.

4. They may have been rejected by families due to sexual and gender identity.

BEHAVIORAL HEALTH:

As a mental health therapist working with the LGBTQ+ community, I have witnessed transgender people being at greater risk of the following: suicide and suicidal thoughts, mood disorders and anxiety, eating disorders and alcohol, tobacco and substance abuse.

If you have picked up this book and work in a physician's office, here is how you can create a safe space and a welcoming environment for the LGBTQ+ community.

1. One small but impactful gesture would be to have safe zone stickers at all entrances

2. Provide gender-neutral bathrooms

3. Signs, brochures and magazines in waiting room related to LGBTQ+ topics

CULTURAL HUMILITY

1. Each client/patient should be approached as an individual with no preconceptions.

2. Meeting clients/patients where they are without judgment will enhance the relationship and avoid perception of stigma.

3. It should NOT be expected that our clients/patients "teach" us, the provider.

Let's talk confidentiality (HIPAA) for a moment. Be careful not to accidently "out" a client or patient. Their gender identity is considered protected health information, and outing a person can be a violation of HIPAA. You may also be placing that person at risk, since there is violence toward transgender people.

Using the wrong name or pronoun may be construed as harassment.

The bottom line: People who identify as trans* are just like everyone else. They want the same things: to be loved, respected and treated like any other human being.

DAYNE BACHMANN, LCSW

Becoming an Ally

Some may wonder how do they go about being an ally?

Your actions can help change the perception people have with individuals who do not adhere to typical societal norms (male/female).

Here are some ways you can further your knowledge on being an ally:

1. Not all transgender people look a certain way, so you can't tell if someone is transgender just by looking at them.

2. Don't assume a transgender person's sexual orientation. Gender and sexual orientation are different. (See page of definitions on sexual orientation and gender identity.)

3. Ask someone what their pronouns are. You can start with your own: "Hi, my name is Dayne, and my pronouns are he/him/his. If you use the wrong pronouns by accident, correct yourself and keep it moving. If you make a big deal about this, the more uncomfortable it is for everyone.

4. Do not ask a transgender person what their "real name" is. This can provoke immense anxiety as it is a part of their life they want to leave behind. Respect the name they ask you to use. Lastly, if you know a person's birth name, do not share this without the person's permission.

5. Always keep confidentiality in mind. Some people do not feel comfortable sharing with others that they are transgender. This information is personal, and it is up to each individual whether they want to share it with others. There can be a lot at stake for the person, such as safety and loss of their job, housing and possibly even friendships.

6. Respect terminology. A transgender individual can use a different term to describe themselves (transgender, non-binary, gender queer etc.) It doesn't matter what label **you** think the person should use, just as you would not want your gender identity to be defined by anyone else but yourself.

7. Be patient with anyone questioning and/or exploring their gender identity as this can take time. They may choose a name and pronoun and, at a later date, change this as they had time to figure it out for themselves. We need to be respectful of everyone's individual process.

8. Do not ask a transgender person about their genitals, sex life and/or surgical status. You wouldn't ask a cisgender person about the appearance or status of their genitals. If a transgender person wants to share this information with you, they will start the conversation about it. Lastly, you would not ask a cisgender person how they have sex, so the

same respect should be extended to transgender people.

9. Back-handed compliments that are actually offensive include the following:

"I would have never known you were transgender. You look so pretty." "You look like a real woman." "She is so gorgeous, I would have never guessed she was transgender." "He is so hot. I'd date him even though he is transgender."

10. Listen to transgender people with an open mind. Check out books, and YouTube channels have good information.

11. Transgender people are not new. They have been around throughout time and history.

12. Know your own limits. Do not be afraid to say I do not know. Seek out appropriate resources that can help you to learn.

If you want to question a transgender person, first, take a moment to self-reflect.

1. Why are you asking the question?

2. Is it something you need to know?

3. Is it a topic you could research on your own?

4. Is it appropriate for the relationship you hold with them?

5. Being curious is natural, but always be respectful.

6. Before asking specific questions, always seek permission from the individual.

7. Do not assume a person is taking specific action in relation to their gender identity (e.g., surgery, hormone therapy).

8. Start with questions like, "Where are you in your journey"? in order to avoid making assumptions.

THE ELEMENTS OF IDENTITY

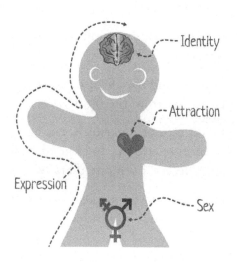

DEFINITIONS

Transgender: When your gender identity is different from the one you were assigned at birth.

Ally: People who support everyone in the LGBTQ+ community.

Asexual: The lack of sexual attraction to others and/or a low interest in sexual activity.

Bisexual: A romantic/sexual attraction toward both females and males.

Cisgender: A person whose gender identity aligns with the sex assigned to them at birth.

Coming Out: A metaphor that is used by the LGBTQ+ community for self-disclosure of their gender identity and/or their sexual orientation.

Dead-naming: The use of someone's former birth name.

Gay: A person who is attracted to the same sex.

Gender Dysphoria: Psychological distress resulting from the incongruence of a person's sex assigned at birth and a person's gender identity.

Gender Expansive: When a person does not identify with being male or female. A person can also express their gender as being both male/female, expressing gender in a different way.

Gender Expression: How a person demonstrates their gender by the way they dress, act, behave and also interact.

Gender Fluid: A person who does not identify themselves as having a fixed gender.

Gender Identity: How an individual perceives themselves. This can be the same or different from the sex they were assigned at birth.

Gender Non-Conforming: Not conforming to gender roles.

Gender Queer: When the gender binary is too limiting. Some gender queer people think of themselves as living between the binary genders. Gender queer enables a person to be flexible to explore their gender.

Gender Transition: A process to match gender identity closer to their outward appearance.

Examples can be social transition (e.g., change clothing, name, pronouns that fit one's gender identity). It can also be a medical transition, such as starting hormone therapy and/or surgery.

Homophobia: Having a dislike or being prejudiced against gay people.

Intersex: A person born with characteristics of both male and female anatomy.

Lesbian: A woman who is romantically, emotionally and/or sexually attracted to another woman.

LGBTQ: This is an acronym for lesbian, gay, bisexual, transgender and queer.

Mis-gendering: Using the wrong name or pronouns to refer to someone.

Non-Binary: A person who does not identify solely as male or female. Some non-binary individuals may identify as both female and male or somewhere in-between.

Outing: When a person shares another person's identity with others without permission.

Pansexual: Having romantic or emotional sexual attraction to people of any gender.

Queer: A person whose sexual orientation is not exclusively heterosexual. Those individuals who identify as lesbian/gay/bisexual can be too limiting. The word queer used to be a slur dating back to about 1972.

Questioning: This term is used by people who are in the process of exploring orientation and identity.

Sex assigned at birth: A label you are given at birth based on external anatomy.

Sexual orientations: Who you are attracted to and want to have a relationship with.

WEBSITES:

The National Center for Transgender Equality
http://www.transequality.org/

Gay and Lesbian Alliance against Defamation (GLAAD)
www.glad.org

Human Rights Campaign (HRC)
www.hrc.org

It gets better project
www.itgetsbetter.org

Parents, families and friends of lesbians and gays
(PFLAG)
www.pflag.org

Suicide Prevention Lifeline. 800-273-8255
www.suicidepreventionlifeline.org

Transgender Law Center
www.transgenderlawcenter.org

Trans lifeline. 877-565-8860
www.translifeline.org

The Trevor Project – A 24/7/365 Lifeline at
866-4-U-TREVOR (866-488-7386), *TrevorChat*,
their online instant messaging option, or *TrevorText*,
a text-based support option. If you are looking for peer
support, you can visit *TrevorSpace* from anywhere in
the world. *www.thetrevorproject.org/get-help-now.*

New Haven Pride Center

LGBTQ Community Center programs and services include social and support groups, social events, information sharing.
https://www.newhavenpridecenter.org

Triangle Community Center

LGBTQ Community Center
Programs and services include social and support groups, youth groups, wellness programs, case management and social events.
https://www.ctpridecenter.org

The Jim Collins Foundation

Provides financial assistance to transgender people for gender-confirming surgeries.
https://jimcollinsfoundation.org

BIOGRAPHY

Dayne Bachmann is a Licensed Clinical Social Worker, Gender Development Therapist and owner of Twin Peaks Counseling Center, New England's premier therapeutic resource for the LGBTQ+ community, located in Derby, Connecticut.

Mr. Bachmann published his first book, SHE HE ME, in 2021. It is a story of his own struggle with gender identity and transgender transition. Along with his formal education, his personal experience enables him to more compassionately and expertly counsel and support his clients and their families.

In addition to being the senior clinician at Twin Peaks Counseling, he leads diversity education and training in gender identity and trans-focal therapy, along with discussions on related ethics for his peers. Presentations and training have included participants of regional leadership programs and the senior medical staff at Griffin Hospital, Planetree Hospital's headquarters.

He holds a master's degree in Social Work from Fordham University.

He resides in Connecticut with his spouse and several furry friends.

He can be reached at http://www.twinpeaks counseling.com/.

Made in the USA
Monee, IL
10 October 2021